6/12

D0403654

A Gift for

_____

Presented by

_____

# I Wish
# I Knew
# That
## Geography

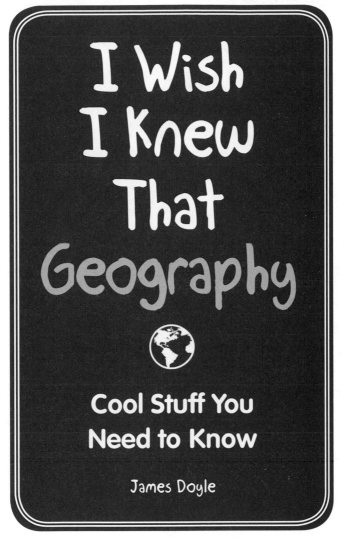

# I Wish I Knew That

# Geography

## Cool Stuff You Need to Know

James Doyle

**Reader's Digest**

The Reader's Digest Association, Inc.

New York, NY / Montreal

**A READER'S DIGEST BOOK**

Copyright © 2012 Michael O'Mara Books Limited

All rights reserved. Unauthorized reproduction, in any manner, is prohibited.

Reader's Digest is a registered trademark of The Reader's Digest Association, Inc.

First published as *Where on Earth?* in Great Britain in 2010 by Michael O'Mara Books Limited, 9 Lion Yard, Tremadoc Road, London SW4 7NQ

**FOR MICHAEL O'MARA BOOKS**
Editors: Sue McMillan, Elizabeth Scoggins, and Sally Pilkington
Maps: David Woodroffe
Illustrator: Andrew Pinder
Designer: Zoe Quayle

**FOR READER'S DIGEST TRADE PUBLISHING**
Consulting Editor: Andrea Chesman
U.S. Project Editor: Kimberly Casey
Manager, English Book Editorial, Reader's Digest Canada: Pamela Johnson
Project Production Coordinator: Rich Kershner
Senior Art Director: George McKeon
Executive Editor, Trade Publishing: Dolores York
Associate Publisher, Trade Publishing: Rosanne McManus
President and Publisher, Trade Publishing: Harold Clarke

Library of Congress Cataloging in Publication Data
Doyle, James, 1972-
I wish I knew that geography : cool stuff you need to know / James Doyle.
    p. cm.
"A Reader's Digest Book."
Includes bibliographical references and index.
ISBN 978-1-60652-347-6
1. Geography--Juvenile literature. I. Title.
G133.D63 2012
910--dc23

                            2011027524

Reader's Digest is committed to both the quality of our products and the service we provide to our customers. We value your comments, so please feel free to contact us:
The Reader's Digest Association, Inc., Adult Trade Publishing, 44 S. Broadway, White Plains, NY 10601

For more Reader's Digest products and information, visit our website:
            www.rd.com (in the United States)
            www.readersdigest.ca (in Canada)

Printed in the United States of America

1 3 5 7 9 10 8 6 4 2

For Oonagh, Conall,
Erin, and Cara

# CONTENTS

# INTRODUCTION:
# WHY IN THE WORLD . . . ?

Have you ever wondered why we don't have kangaroos in North America? Or why earthquakes happen more frequently in some parts of the world than others? Or why some hot places are deserts and some are rain forests? And why do people talk about rain forests all the time, anyway? These are questions that geographers think about all the time. Geography is the science that explains where in the world things are and how they got there. Geography looks at the whole world and brings together geology, meteorology, history, and biology to help describe the world.

The earth is constantly changing. Did you know that mountains actually grow? New islands form, too. And floods and tsunamis (giant ocean waves) change the surface of the planet. Why does this happen?

Whew! Lots of questions. Let's take a look at the always-changing earth from the inside out, and then look at the oceans and the seven continents, the mountains, the rivers—how to find it all on a map. Words in bold will help you pay attention to key terms as you go. Soon you will be able to answer anyone who asks, "What is the difference between an ocean and a sea?" or "Where on earth is the longest river?"—and lots more.

Impress your friends, your parents, and your teachers with all the cool new stuff you know! The world is at your fingertips.

# WELCOME TO
# PLANET EARTH

# HOME SWEET HOME

Earth, the planet we call home, is one of a group of eight planets that move around the sun. These planets in order of closeness to the sun are: **Mercury, Venus, Earth, Mars, Jupiter, Saturn, Uranus,** and **Neptune**. Together, they make up the **solar system**.

Until recently, **Pluto** was considered the ninth planet in the solar system. Pluto still exists, but since it is smaller than the earth's moon, scientists decided it should be called a "dwarf planet." (Pluto isn't the only dwarf planet. There are also Ceres and Eris, not to mention plenty of asteroids, comets, and meteoroids orbiting the sun.)

Earth is a special planet because on it there is life—you, me, and all the people, animals, plants, and microorganisms. Scientists think Earth may be the *only* planet with living creatures in the whole **universe** (all of outer space, including all the stars, planets, moons, comets, asteroids, you name it).

### It's a Small World after All

The earth feels like a huge place, but in fact it is only the fifth largest planet in the solar system. Jupiter is the biggest—its diameter is 11 times greater than that of Earth's.

# WHAT IS THE WORLD MADE OF?

The earth is a **terrestrial planet**, which means it is mostly made from rock rather than gas. It has three main layers. These layers are kind of like the layers of a piece of fruit, with a thin crust (or skin), thick center, and core.

**The Crust.** The outer layer of the earth—where people, animals, and plants live—is the **crust.** It is the thinnest layer, measuring from about 5 miles (8 km) thick under the oceans to about 25 miles (40 km) thick in places under land. Two types of volcanic rocks, granite and basalt, make up most of the earth's crust.

**The Mantle.** Under the crust lies the **mantle,** which is about 1,800 miles (2,900 km) thick. The mantle is made up of thick, gooey, partially melted rock called **magma.** Magma isn't solid because the temperature of the mantle is about 3,600°F (2,000°C)—and that's hot enough to melt rock.

Crust

**The Core.** The earth's core is so deep below the surface that scientists aren't entirely sure what it is made of—although they believe the core contains mostly two metals: iron and nickel.

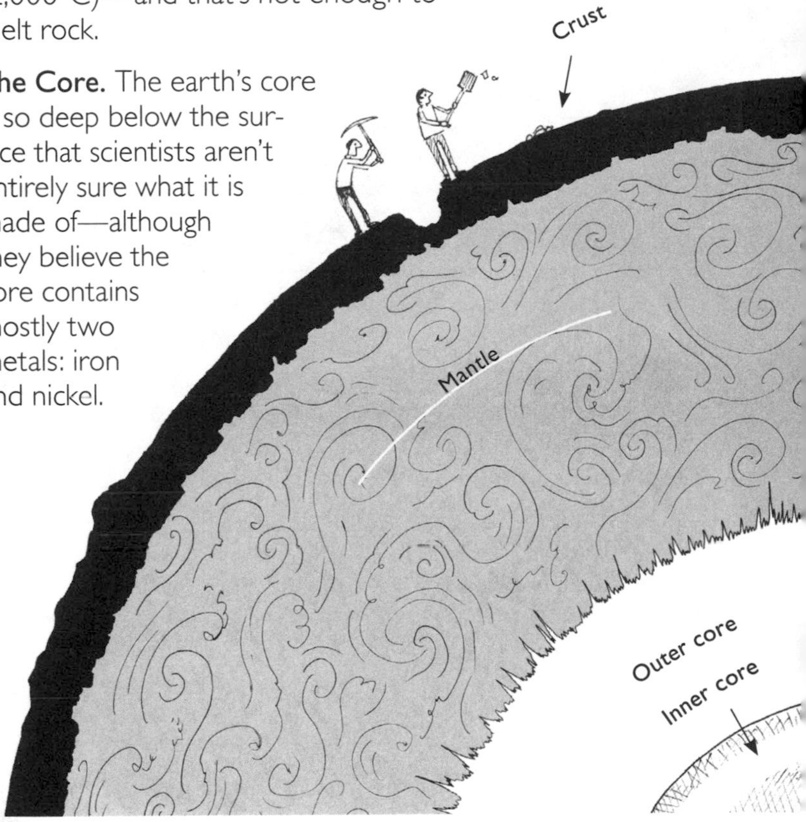

Mantle

Outer core

Inner core

They think it is extremely hot, with temperatures greater than 12,600°F (7,000°C). The **outer core** is about 1,400 miles (2,250 km) thick and is liquid. The **inner core** is about 1,600 miles (2,600 km) in diameter (all the way across). It is probably scorching hot there, too, but scientists think the inner core is solid because the weight of all the other layers press down on it.

### Journey to the Center of the Earth

The distance from the earth's surface to the center is about 4,000 miles (6,400 km). But you could never actually make a journey to the center of the earth—you'd either be fried to a crisp in the scorching heat or crushed to death by the pressure of the layers of rock in the crust and mantle.

# CONTINENTS AND OCEANS

A continent is a large landmass. It is thought that at one time (about 250 million years ago), all the land on the earth was part of one big landmass that split apart into seven continents: **North America, South America, Europe, Africa, Asia, Australia/Oceania,** and **Antarctica.** Europe and Asia form a single landmass divided by the Ural Mountains and the Caspian and Black seas. Europe and Asia are the only continents that are so tightly joined. Some geographers say the two should be called "Eurasia" or "Europe/Asia." The combination continent many people agree on is Australia/Oceania, which includes many of the Pacific Islands as well as Australia itself.

Continents account for just one-third of the earth's surface. Oceans cover the rest of the planet's crust, which is why the earth looks blue from outer space. There are five oceans:

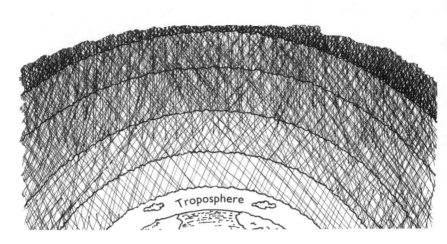

Troposphere

the **Pacific, Atlantic, Indian, Southern,** and **Arctic.** Some people call the Southern Ocean the "Antarctic Ocean."

# AWESOME ATMOSPHERE

The **atmosphere** wraps the planet in a thin layer of gases, which protect the earth from the sun's burning hot temperatures. The atmosphere of the earth is made up mostly of the gases oxygen, nitrogen, and argon. There are also trace (small) amounts of other gases and little particles, like dust, water, and pollen. The part of the atmosphere where we live and breathe is called the **troposphere.** This is also where the earth's weather happens.

# THE HOT AND THE COLD OF IT

Planet Earth is a spinning ball of rock. It takes 24 hours—one day—for the earth to complete one spin, or rotation. As it

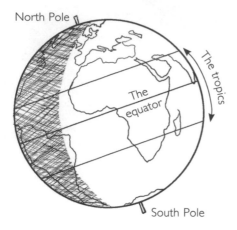

spins, the earth is also moving in an **orbit** (a circular path) around the sun. Radiation from the sun heats the planet, but it hits the planet unevenly. An area around the middle of the planet, called the **tropics,** which includes the **equator,** receives more heat than the parts at the top and bottom, which are known as the **Arctic Circle** and the **Antarctic zone.**

That uneven heating explains why we find warm, wet, tropical rainforests and hot, dry deserts near the equator and why polar bears and penguins call the frozen lands at the North and South poles home. Temperatures would be even more extreme in these areas if there weren't some helpful conditions in the atmosphere.

### Earth's Air-Conditioning System

Heat from the sun moves from warmer parts of the earth to cooler areas by the constant movement of ocean currents, winds, and big storms, such as hurricanes. Without this movement, the tropics would be too hot and the poles too cold for most forms of life to survive, and maybe even too hot and cold for people! So currents too strong to swim against and wind that blows dirt in your eyes are good things—sort of.

# THE REASON FOR SEASONS

Even though we think of the North Pole as up, the earth actually tilts to one side as it travels around the sun. As the earth moves, different parts of the planet get more sunshine at different times of the year.

When it is winter in the North, the **Northern Hemisphere** (the northern half of the planet) is tilted away from the sun. Because the Northern Hemisphere is farther from the sun at this time, not as much heat and light reaches it, and the weather feels cooler. Meanwhile, it is summer in the **Southern Hemisphere** because that half of the planet gets more hours of sunlight each day, and the weather feels warmer. As the earth continues on its orbit, the Northern Hemisphere starts to get more sunlight each day, the weather heats up, and summer arrives. That is when winter begins in the Southern Hemisphere.

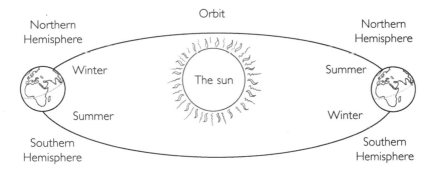

## Earth Fact Sheet

| | |
|---:|:---|
| Age | 4.5 to 4.6 billion years |
| Distance from the Sun | 93,000,000 miles (150,000,000 km) |
| Distance from the Moon | 239,000 miles (384,000 km) |
| Distance around the equator (the middle) | 25,000 miles (40,075 km) |
| Surface area | 196,938,500 square miles (510,065,700 km²) |
| Surface area of land | 57,500,000 square miles (148,940,000 km²) |
| Surface area of ocean | 139,400,000 square miles (361,132, 000 km²) |
| Mass | 13,131,920,000,000,000,000,000,000 pounds or 6,000 billion, billion tons |

# POLAR OPPOSITES

The exact **North Pole,** located in the Arctic Circle, is the one point on the planet where you cannot go any farther north. If you stood at the North Pole and walked in any direction, you would be heading south. Of course, you'd actually be walking on a floating sheet of ice. At the North Pole, and the area around it, there is no land at all—just hundreds of miles of ice.

The exact **South Pole,** located in the Antarctic, is the most southern point on the planet, so if you stood at the South Pole and walked in any direction, you would be heading north. Unlike the North Pole, the South Pole is located on land, but it's buried under ice that is more than 1¼ miles (2 km) thick. What else sets the poles apart? Their seasons are entirely opposite due to the tilt of the earth's axis (see page 17). So on a balmy summer's day in the Arctic, when it might be as "warm" as 32°F (0°C), it's a teeth-chattering winter's day in Antarctica, where the temperatures can reach as low as −56°F (−49°C).

## It's Been a Long Day . . .

Did you know that at the North and South poles, a summer "day" can last up to six months and a winter's "night" can be just as long? As the earth spins, the top of the planet, the North Pole, points at the sun for six months and then points away from it for the next six months. This means that when the Arctic is bathed in summer sunshine, the Antarctic is plunged into a long, dark winter, and vice versa.

Even though the poles get so many hours of sunshine, their summers are still very cold and temperatures rarely climb above freezing. This is because the sun is always low in the sky; its rays are weakened because they have to travel farther to reach the poles than they do to reach the equator. The poles are also covered in white ice, which reflects heat back into the atmosphere.

### Solid Ice?

Until recently, many explorers and scientists thought the Arctic, like Antarctica, was a landmass covered by ice. In 1958 a submarine journeyed beneath the ice cap and came out the other side, proving that there is no land at all and that the Arctic is nothing but ice.

# Polar Bear versus Penguin

Polar bears live in the Arctic, and penguins live in the Antarctic and parts of the Southern Hemisphere. Both need cold weather to survive, but which animal can withstand the toughest climate?

**The Polar Bear.** This animal is the largest meat eater living on land. It is well-suited to temperatures below zero and can travel over snow and ice easily. The polar bear is a great swimmer, too. A thick layer of fat beneath the skin acts like thermal underwear to keep the polar bear warm and helps it float in icy water. It can smell food—seals and other marine animals—over great distances and is armed with powerful jaws and large claws. The polar bear must survive winter temperatures of −22°F (−30°C) in the Arctic, but that's nothing . . .

**The Penguin.** The emperor penguin is the largest species of penguin. Like the polar bear, it is a super swimmer and has a thick layer of fat under its skin to keep it warm. But that's not what makes it the winner of this polar contest. The emperor penguin breeds during the bone-chilling Antarctic winter. While the female penguin goes in search of food, the male protects their egg through the harshest winter on Earth. He faces temperatures of −76°F (−60°C), fierce winds, and four months without sunlight, food, or water. He huddles with other males on the polar ice, waiting for the mother penguin to return, the egg to hatch, and the mother penguin to take over and feed the chick. That may make the penguin the winner in a contest of polar bear versus penguin. What do you think?

## Planet Earth's Designer Sunglasses

Believe it or not, the ice, snow, and freezing temperatures at the planet's poles help keep the rest of the world at a comfortable temperature range. The icy poles are bright white in color and this maximizes their **albedo.** The word albedo (pronounced al-bee-doh) is used to describe how reflective the surfaces on Earth are. Earth's oceans and dark soils aren't very good at reflecting the sun's rays, so they have a very low albedo—about 10 percent. This means they absorb more heat from the sun than they reflect. Fresh snow has a high albedo—around 85 percent or more. So large, icy areas, such as the North and South poles act like giant mirrors, reflecting most of the sunlight they receive back into space, helping the planet stay cool. If there were no ice at the earth's poles, the planet would be a much warmer place.

## The Warm Pole

The Arctic is the warmer of the two poles. Its temperature ranges from 32°F (0°C) in the summer to a very cold −22°F (−30 °C) in the winter. The Antarctic is much colder. The average summer temperature there is around −22°F (−30°C), and in the winter it can reach below −76°F (−60°C). The coldest temperature ever recorded on Earth was −128°F (−89°C) at Vostok Station, Antarctica, in July 1983.

# CLIMATES ARE COMPLICATED

**Weather** is the hour-to-hour or day-to-day state of the atmosphere. **Climate** describes the state of the atmosphere over a much longer period (usually at least 30 years).

If climate were just a result of how close to (or far away from) the equator or the North or South poles a certain place is, climate would be easy to understand. But the picture is complicated by whether the land is mountainous, whether it is near an ocean, where the wind comes from, and more.

**Prevailing Winds.** Places nearer the equator receive more sunlight and are much warmer than places nearer the poles. The heat causes air currents that rise and drive the general circulation of the atmosphere, moving heat away from the equator toward the poles. The wind belts that form are sometimes called the **prevailing winds.** They blow east-west more often than north-south due to the rotation of the earth.

**Land Features. Topography** is the word we use to describe whether there are mountains or valleys or flat open land. Mountain ranges act like walls, blocking the movement of air. In North America, the coastal mountain ranges and the Sierras block prevailing winds from the west that carry moisture from the Pacific Ocean. The warm air hits the mountain barrier and rises. As it rises, it cools. As it cools, it can't hold as much moisture, so rain falls. So on the west side of the mountain, lots of rain falls, but on the east side of the mountain . . . not so much. Sometimes deserts form on the dry sides of mountains.

**Elevation.** As you hike up a mountain, you feel the air temperature drop and maybe have to add more layers of clothing. That's because as air rises, temperatures fall. On some mountains, the tops are covered with ice and snow all year long. The higher the **elevation** of a place, the cooler the climate. Mount Kilimanjaro (located in the United Republic of Tanzania) lies about 200 miles (320 km)

**Whether the Weather?**

Whether the weather be hot,
Or whether the weather be not,
We'll weather the weather,
Whatever the weather,
Whether we like it or not.

## A Brief Time Line of the Earth

| | |
|---|---|
| **4.6 billion years ago** | Earth formed, along with the other planets |
| **3.7 billion years ago** | Earth's crust solidified |
| **3.5 billion years ago** | First life appeared in oceans |
| **1 billion years ago** | Plants and fungi appeared |
| **600 million years** | Simple animals started to appear |
| **500 million years** | Fish and early amphibians appeared |
| **475 million years** | Plants moved onto land |
| **300 million years** | Reptiles evolved on land |
| **245 million years ago** | Age of Dinosaurs began |
| **200 million years** | Mammals appeared |
| **150 million years ago** | Supercontinent broke up and birds took to the air |
| **65 million years ago** | Age of Dinosaurs ended, with mass extinctions |
| **2.5 million years ago** | Early ancestors of man made an appearance |
| **100,000 years ago** | First Homo sapiens appeared |
| **10,000 years ago** | Recorded human history began |

Note: The dates above are only estimates, and new information continually forces science to revise the "facts."

south of the equator, well within the tropics, but ice and snow cover the summit all year long.

**Land versus Oceans.** The oceans absorb heat far more slowly than land. During the summer, bodies of water are cooler than the adjoining land, which is why swimming in the ocean or in a big lake is so refreshing. But in winter the big waters are warmer, and that keeps the land they border warmer as well. Also there are warm ocean currents, such as the Gulf Stream in the Atlantic, for example, that help keep the weather in places like England and Cape Cod, Massachusetts, warmer than it would be otherwise. Coastal regions generally experience mild and humid **maritime climates,** while the interiors of large landmasses boast **continental climates,** with warmer summers and colder winters. The summers stay cooler and the winters are milder in Portland, Oregon, for example, than in Minneapolis, Minnesota, even though the two cities are located in nearly the same latitude (see page 59).

# THE EARTH NEVER STOPS CHANGING

# CRACKS IN THE CRUST

Most of the time change happens slowly on planet Earth, over periods of millions of years. Then there are changes—like earthquakes or the eruption of volcanoes—that happen in an instant.

The earth's crust is one of those changeable parts. Many pieces, called **plates,** fit together to form the crust, like a giant jigsaw puzzle. There are seven enormous plates, and many smaller ones. The study of how these plates move is called **plate tectonics.** The plates float on the partially melted mantle (see page 13), which moves them slowly over the earth's surface. Most of the **boundaries** (edges) are under the sea and move only a few inches a year, but they do move.

## Drifting Apart

Today the land is divided into continents and islands, but about 250 million years ago, all the land was joined together

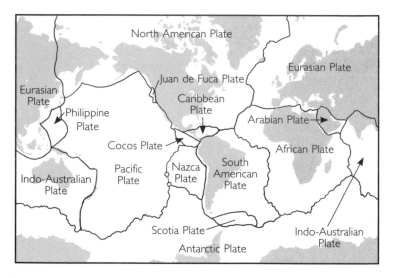

as one big continent called **Pangaea** (pronounced pan-gee-a), which means "all lands" in ancient Greek. It was surrounded by a huge ocean called **Panthalassa,** which means "all seas."

A German geographer named Alfred Wegener (1880–1930) noticed that on a map the shape of the east coast of South America looked as if it fit into the west coast of Africa. Did South America break off from Africa? Wegener asked himself. When he watched icebergs drifting out to sea in Greenland, Wegener realized that continents could be moving, too. Most people thought he was crazy at the time, but in the 1960s scientists proved his theory.

One piece of evidence was the fossilized remains of the mesosaurus, a dinosaur that lived about 300 million years ago. This dinosaur was found only in Africa and South America, two continents separated by a huge ocean—and this particular dinosaur couldn't swim or fly. But what if those continents had once been attached? Problem solved! Another puzzle: You can dig below the ice in certain spots to find coal in

Antarctica. Coal is made from decaying plants. No plants can live in Antarctica these days because it is just too cold and dry there. So either the weather at the South Pole has changed a lot (unlikely given the distance from the equator) or the continent of Antarctica moved from a warm spot on the globe. Bingo! More evidence for continental drift.

# CONTINENTS ON THE MOVE

The world has changed a lot in the last 250 million years because the tectonic plates move, carrying the continents with them. These maps show how the continents are thought to have moved during this time.

**250 Million Years Ago.** The continents were joined in one enormous landmass, called Pangaea.

**200 Million Years Ago.** Pangaea started to split into two giant continents—**Laurasia** in the north and **Gondwana** in the south.

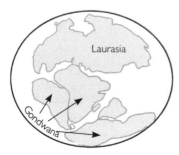

**135 Million Years Ago.** The two giant continents started to split once more as Gondwana divided into Africa and South America, separated by the Atlantic Ocean. India broke off from Africa to form a separate island continent and drifted north.

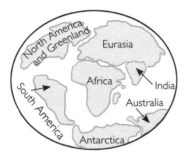

**40 Million Years Ago.** The continents began to look as they do today. Australia/Oceania and Antarctica started drifting apart. India collided with Eurasia. North America and Greenland shifted west, splitting away from Eurasia. Later, Greenland became an island when rising sea levels cut it off from North America.

The world has not stopped changing because the earth's tectonic plants still move. Some plates are moving toward each other on a collision course. As these plates bump into each other, one plate gets pushed under the other, the rock melts, and it becomes part of the earth's mantle. These boundaries are called **destructive boundaries** because land is destroyed.

At the same time, new land is created all the time. When plates pull away from one another, molten rock, or magma, is released into the gap, hardening to form new land. These points are known as **constructive boundaries.** Most of these points are located under the sea.

# ENORMOUS EARTHQUAKES

Earthquakes take place where two tectonic plates meet, called a **fault plane.** When two plates slip past each other, the rock and magma below the planet's surface shakes and rolls. Sometimes you can hardly feel this movement, and sometimes it can destroy whole cities.

Although many plate boundaries are under the oceans, there are some on land. The San Andreas Fault, for example, stretches for more than 560 miles (900 km) along the west coast of the United States, passing through two large cities, San Francisco and Los Angeles. There are frequent earthquakes along this fault.

## Whose Fault Is It?

More than 80 percent of all earthquakes happen in the **Ring of Fire,** an area in the Pacific Ocean that is famous for its volcanoes and earthquakes. It's the shakiest place on the planet! But earthquakes can happen wherever plate boundaries come together. While most plates move past each other, some plate boundaries get stuck. And although the plate edges are stuck, the rest of the plate continues to move. The energy that would usually help the plates slide past one another is stored up, so when the faults finally slip apart, the stored-up energy is released, causing the land to shake violently. The energy radiates in all directions from the fault in what are known as **seismic waves.** When the waves reach the earth's surface, they are felt as vibrations. These may be anything from a little wobble to huge tremors. Seismic waves are measured by seismographs that assign a number based on the **Richter scale,** developed by a man named Charles Richter (1900–1985). Each whole number on the scale represents a tenfold increase in the size of an earthquake, so a medium-size earthquake might measure 5.3 on the Richter scale, but one that measures 6.3 would be considered a strong earthquake because it is 10 times greater. The strongest earthquake ever measured took place in Chile in 1960; it measured 9.5 on the Richter scale.

## How Shocking!

Some earthquakes begin with **foreshocks,** or little tremors, that happen in advance of the main shock. The main shock is the largest and most violent part and is followed by smaller earthquakes called **aftershocks.** If the main shock is really big, the aftershocks can go on for days, months, or even years.

# PRESSURE POINTS

Earthquakes are in the news a lot. What makes them so dangerous is that no one can say exactly when or where the next one will happen.

**Pacific Ring of Fire.** The earthquakes that occur frequently in Japan and California are all part of the Ring of Fire, a horseshoe-shaped fault line that stretches from Indonesia and the Philippines, past China to the Aleutian Islands in the United States, then down through Alaska, the Pacific Northwest, down the San Andreas Fault to Mexico, and into South America.

**Alpine-Himalayan Zone.** The Alpine-Himalayan zone goes through India, Tibet, and China, down to Myanmar and across to the Middle East, and then over to the Mediterranean.

**East Africa Rift.** Africa is ripping apart along a 2,400-mile (3,862 km) crack that stretches from the Red Sea to Mozambique. This big split started in the north some 25 million years ago and has been creeping south, apparently on the way to splitting the African Plate into two new tectonic plates.

**The Caribbean.** The Caribbean Plate is small, but it borders the North American Plate, the South American Plate, the Nazca Plate, and the Cocos Plate (see page 26). Where there are boundaries between plates, you can expect a lot of earthquake action, like the devastating 2009 earthquake in Haiti.

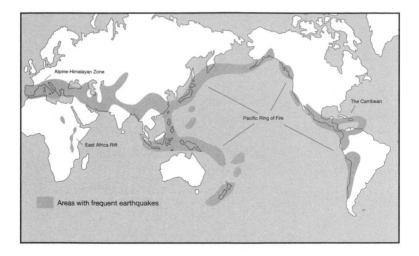

Alpine-Himalayan Zone

East Africa Rift

Pacific Ring of Fire

The Carribean

Areas with frequent earthquakes

# EARTH-SHATTERING EFFECTS

Major earthquakes can be deadly, causing buildings to collapse and roads and bridges to be destroyed. The shaking can make the ground feel like jelly, damaging electric and gas lines, which cause fires. Landslides and avalanches can also be triggered by earthquakes. If the **epicenter** (center of the earthquake) is located in the ocean, an earthquake can create a huge wave, called a **tsunami**.

## Towering Tsunamis

A tsunami is triggered when water in the ocean is moved violently. This sets off a ripple effect, and the waves travel across the oceans. In open water, the waves travel fast and a great distance apart, but as they reach shallower water, they slow down and pile up to form a wall of water up to 130 feet (40 m) high. In December 2004, a huge tsunami struck in Indonesia, Southeast Asia, after an earthquake in the Indian

Ocean measuring more than 9.0 on the Richter scale. The tsunami struck across a huge part of the globe, including Thailand, Sri Lanka, Indonesia, and the coast of Somalia, in Africa. More than 200,000 people were killed, and more than 1.5 million people were left homeless. A tsunami in March 2011 followed an earthquake off the east coast of Japan, which measured 9.0 on the Richter scale. The tsunami caused a partial meltdown of a nuclear power plant, killed an estimated 25,000 people, and left many homeless.

# VOLCANIC ACTION

Volcanoes are destructive when they erupt and spew molten lava or hot, volcanic ash. But at the same time, they are famous for being builders of mountains and islands.

## Nasty Eruptions

A volcano is the point at which magma, or liquid rock, from the earth's mantle, erupts through the ground. Pressure forces either magma or hot volcanic ash out of the ground through a **vent,** or hole, in the earth's surface.

## Molten Mountains

Volcanoes can form anywhere on Earth, even on the ocean floor! They usually form along the edges of tectonic plates, where the different sections of the planet's surface push toward or pull away from each other. Magma builds up in huge underground chambers and erupts as **lava,** the name for magma once it is aboveground. Lava is destructive and dangerously hot, like 1,290°F (700°C) hot, and can even reach a temperature of 2,280°F (1,250°C). It can be thick and slow-moving like jam, runny like melted ice cream, or any consistency in between. As it cools, lava hardens and forms new rock, including **pumice** (pronounced puh-miss). Over time, different volcano shapes build up depending on the viscosity, or thickness, of the lava. The thickness varies according to the type of melted rock and how much pressure is inside the volcano.

# ATTACK OF THE VOLCANO

Lava flows can destroy pretty much anything in their path, but there's even more to the dangers of volcanoes. Here are just a few of them:

**Lahars.** These volcanic mudflows of ash and debris mix with water to form deadly mudslides. The water can be a result of heavy rain just after an eruption, or when eruptions melt ice on a snow-capped volcano. On steep slopes a lahar can travel at speeds fast enough to knock down trees and bury houses. **Mount Ranier** in Washington State is the type of volcano likely to generate a lahar flow, but the last time that happened was about 500 years ago.

**Dust Clouds.** Volcanoes can spread dust clouds across the globe, blocking out the sun and lowering temperatures. If the layers of ash are very thick, the temperature can be lowered for years. In 1815 **Mount Tambora** in Indonesia erupted, sending so much dust into the atmosphere that 1816 was known as "the year without a summer" in parts of North America.

**Flooding.** Volcanic eruptions can also cause flooding—especially when they occur underwater. They can create giant waves called tsunamis (see page 33). In 1883 the eruption of **Krakatau,** in Indonesia, created a wave that was 130 feet (40 m) high. It is estimated that the Krakatau tsunami killed more than 36,000 people.

## Volcanoes Up Close

Some volcanoes that aren't in imminent danger of exploding and killing visitors have turned into tourist attractions. Here's some you can visit:

- Mount St. Helens National Volcanic Monument, Washington State
- Volcanoes National Park, Hawaii (Kilauea and Mauna Loa volcanoes)
- Arenal Volcano, Costa Rica
- Popocatepetl National Park, Mexico
- Santa Maria/Santiaguito Volcano, Guatemala
- Vesuvius, Mount Etna, and Stromboli volcanoes, Italy
- Kilimanjaro, Oldoinya Lengai, Meru volcanoes, Tanzania
- Fuji Five Lake Region, Japan (Mount Fuji)

## Hot Spots!

**Hot spots** are superheated areas below the earth's crust. The high temperatures cause the crust to melt, allowing magma to escape and build volcanoes—even away from plate margins. A hot spot can keep a volcano erupting for centuries, but as the earth's tectonic plates shift, the land moves away from the hot spot and its magma, so the volcano becomes **dormant,** or resting, and cannot erupt.

Some volcanic places, such as Iceland and New Zealand, have **geysers,** or hot springs. These produce hot water and jets of steam that can be used to heat homes and provide electricity. They are also popular tourist destinations. Volcanic eruptions also produce mineral-rich rock, creating some of the world's most fertile farmland.

# CLIMATE CHANGE

These days many people worry about global warming. Most scientists understand that actions of humans are causing global temperatures to rise. Global warming and chilling have happened before on planet Earth, and these changes in temperature changed the land.

Periods of cold are known as **ice ages,** and they usually last millions or tens of millions of years. The latest ice age began about 2.5 million years ago. During that time, giant ice sheets called **glaciers** advanced and retreated many times in North America and Europe. During each ice age, the average temperatures around the world dropped. The areas around the equator stayed warm, but the rest of the planet was very, very cold. Many species of plants and animals couldn't adapt to the changing climate and became extinct.

SURELY THIS MUST BE THE TOP?

Those giant glaciers did a good job of bulldozing the land to make the five Great Lakes that border the United States and Canada. They also created the Finger Lakes in New York State, Walden Pond in Massachusetts, and any number of lakes in North America and Canada. The glaciers also carved out the Colorado, Missouri, and Mississippi rivers. As glaciers move, they pick up large amounts of rock and soil and then drop their loads in new places.

Glaciers lock up a lot of water. As more and more water freezes, sea levels drop, and land bridges appear between continents and islands. Those land bridges allowed early man to migrate to new lands, which is how people came to occupy North and South America and Australia.

The worry with global warming today is how it will affect the earth in the long term. Global warming will cause storms to increase in power, which increases the potential damage from storms, especially flooding. If the polar ice caps melt, sea levels will rise, and islands and coastal land will be submerged under water. Florida's Everglades could be

Glacial ice carves away the rock.

Cirque

Glacier

A lip forms as some debris is deposited at the edge of the cirque.

Rocky debris scours away the base, forming a hollow.

completely submerged. In some areas, such as low-lying islands in the Pacific, a 3-foot (1-m) rise in sea levels would be catastrophic. Low-lying countries, such as Bangladesh off the coast of India and the Netherlands, a country in Europe, are also at risk, as are parts of southeast England. If this happened, the world map could look very different, with the shape of some countries and continents changed forever. Some islands like the Maldive Islands in the Indian Ocean could disappear off the map completely.

If *all* the polar ice were to melt (which would probably never happen), scientists think that the sea level all over the world would rise about 230 feet (70 m). This could create some big changes in how maps look. The United States could be split by a newly formed Mississippi Sea, which would connect the Great Lakes with the Gulf of Mexico!

The earth—it keeps changing.

# OCEANS IN MOTION

# OCEANS AND SEAS

Oceans cover more than 70 percent of the earth's surface and are home to some of the deepest valleys and tallest mountains in the world. They have a lot of influence on the weather and are jam-packed with life—yet much about them remains a mystery.

The earth's oceans are all connected and form one gigantic body of water, which is sometimes known as the global ocean. Geographers have divided the global ocean into five enormous oceans. In order of size, these are the Pacific, the Atlantic, the Indian, the Southern—or Antarctic—and the Arctic.

The five oceans include many smaller parts known as **seas.** Most seas are partly enclosed by land, but each sea is part of one of the oceans. One of the largest seas is the South China Sea in Asia. It is more than 1,158,000 square miles (3,000,000 km²) in size and is part of the Pacific Ocean. Another word that describes a part of an ocean is *gulf.* The Gulf of Mexico and the Caribbean Sea, for example, are both parts of the Atlantic Ocean. Some inland saltwater lakes, such as the Dead Sea in Israel, are also called seas, because the water in them is so salty.

The table on the right tells you where in the world you'll find the earth's oceans and how big they are.

## Never Peaceful Pacific

Ferdinand Magellan, the first explorer to sail around the world, named the Pacific in 1519. *Pacifica* means peaceful in Portuguese, Magellan's native language. But the Pacific is anything but a peaceful ocean.

What follows are some fascinating facts about this important body of water.

## Our Oceans

| OCEAN | AREA | WHERE IN THE WORLD? |
|-------|------|---------------------|
| Pacific | 60,610,00 sq. mi. (155,557,000 sq km) | Pacific Ocean |
| Atlantic | 29,638,000 sq. mi. (76,762,000 sq km) | Atlantic Ocean |
| Indian | 16,979,000 sq. mi. (68,556,000 sq km) | Indian Ocean |
| Southern | 7,848,000 sq. mi. (20,327,000 sq km) | South Pole / Southern Ocean |
| Arctic | 5,427,000 sq. mi. (14,056,000 sq km) | North Pole / Arctic Ocean |

## Tsunami Trouble

Earthquakes under the ocean sometimes generate huge waves called tsunamis (see page 33). When a tsunami hits land, there is only one thing to do—run! To make evacuation easier, an international warning system alerts coastal areas of potential tsunamis as soon as they begin to form in the ocean. Scientists constantly monitor the sea for earthquake activity and changes in sea level that indicate a tsunami is coming.

- The Pacific is the largest ocean; it covers more than a third of the earth's surface. It contains more than half of the earth's water.

- The Pacific is home to the **Pacific Ring of Fire,** an area of intense earthquake and volcanic activity. More than 75 percent of the world's volcanoes lie within this ring.

- The deepest spot on the surface of the earth, the **Mariana Trench,** is located in the Pacific Ocean, just east of the island of Guam. The bottommost point of the trench, called **Challenger Deep,** is about 36,000 feet (11,000 m) below sea level. If you were able to pick up and move Mount Everest, the highest mountain on Earth, and place it on this spot, it wouldn't even break the surface of the water; there would be about 1 mile (1.6 km) of ocean concealing it.

- The greatest amount of the world's fish supply is caught in the Pacific Ocean.

- Hurricanes that start in the Pacific are called **typhoons.**

### The Mountainous Atlantic

The second largest ocean, the Atlantic Ocean, separates the Americas from Europe and Africa. It is the most mountainous ocean because undersea volcanoes constantly build new mountains under the water along the **Mid-Atlantic Ridge.** This is the longest mountain range in the world, snaking along the ocean floor for 7,000 miles (11,265 km).

Here are important facts about this vast ocean.

• The Atlantic was formed when the supercontinent Pangaea broke apart (see page 27). As the western and eastern landmasses drew apart, a great rift was formed, creating the Atlantic Ocean basin.

• **Hurricanes** form in the Atlantic. From June 1 to November 30, tropical storms originate off the coast of Africa and cross the Atlantic, taking up vast amounts of moisture. The storms blow over the Caribbean, coastal areas of the Gulf of Mexico, and the southern Atlantic coast of the United States with damaging winds, devastating amounts of rain, and **storm surges** (water levels far higher than the expected tides).

• Waters from many of the world's largest rivers flow into the Atlantic, including the **Amazon, Congo,** and **Niger** rivers. The **Nile River** flows into the Mediterranean Sea, which is part of the Atlantic. The Atlantic is the **saltiest ocean** because so much river water, which carries dissolved minerals, flows into it.

- The largest island in the Atlantic Ocean is **Greenland.**

- The newest island in the Atlantic is **Surtsey,** formed off the coast of Iceland in 1963.

## Tropical Indian Ocean

The Indian Ocean surrounds India and stretches from Africa to Australia.

What else do we know about this tropical body of water?

- The Indian Ocean is the warmest ocean. It lies mostly below the equator. The **Arabian Sea, Persian Gulf,** and **Red Sea** are all part of the Indian Ocean.

- Forty percent of the world's offshore oil drilling takes place in the Indian Ocean.

- The Bay of Bengal is sometimes called **Cyclone Alley** because

### Sunken Continent

Submerged in the Indian Ocean is a microcontinent (small continent) called the Kerguelen Plateau. A series of large volcanic eruptions beginning 110 million years ago started its formation. Rocks found on the plateau are similar to ones found in Australia and India, suggesting they were once connected. Evidence also suggests that the plateau was above sea level for some of its history, perhaps covered by dense forest. The plateau finally sank underwater about 20 million years ago and is now 1 to 1¼ miles (1 to 2 km) below sea level.

of all the storms that begin there. (A cyclone is a type of tropical storm.)

- An earthquake under the Indian Ocean caused the disastrous **Indonesian tsunami** of 2004. It generated waves recorded at a height of 49 feet (15 m).

- Changing air pressure systems over the Indian Ocean trigger the famous **monsoon** (rainy) **seasons** of Asia.

- The Maldive Islands, 8 feet (2.4 m) above sea level at their highest point, are expected to be the first casualties of rising sea levels caused by global warming.

## Penguins' Southern Ocean Paradise

Some geographers call this body of water the Antarctic Ocean. Others think that it shouldn't be an ocean at all! Instead they want the Atlantic and Pacific oceans to claim this area of the globe. However, *most* geographers agree to make space on the map for the Southern Ocean, which extends north from the coast of Antarctica to 60° south latitude. But even this aspect of the ocean provokes fighting. Some Australian geographers say it extends all the way to Australia's shore. Work it out, people!

Here is even more surprising information about this chilliest of oceans.

- The Southern Ocean has the coldest waters of all the oceans.

- It is the **least salty** of the oceans.

- Penguins like to swim in the Southern Ocean.

- The **Antarctic Circumpolar Current** (ACC) flows west to east around Antarctica and is the strongest ocean current in the world. This current prevents warm waters from

## Why Is the Ocean Salty?

Oceans are salty because fresh water flows into them. Okay, that answer doesn't *seem* to make sense, but fresh water flow is the major contributor of salt. The original oceans were probably only slightly salty. Over millions of years, rivers flowed over the newly formed land, carving out canyons, dissolving mountains, and picking up lots of dissolved minerals—including salt. These dissolved minerals all eventually flow into the ocean. Meanwhile, the sun heats the ocean surface, causing water to evaporate. What's left behind are those dissolved minerals—a cycle that continues today. The Atlantic Ocean has the greatest amount of river water flowing into it, so it is the saltiest of the oceans.

reaching Antarctica and enables that continent to maintain its huge ice sheet.

### Icy Arctic Ocean

Much of the Arctic Ocean lies north of the Arctic Circle. It is a sea of ice but that may be changing due to global warming.

Take a look at these fascinating facts.

- The Arctic Ocean is the smallest ocean.

- It is the shallowest ocean.

- Polar bears swim and hunt in the Arctic Ocean.

- It is bordered by North America, Europe, and Asia.

- During winter, the Arctic Ocean is almost completely covered in sea ice.

- The North Pole is located in the middle of the Arctic Ocean.

- For centuries, explorers tried to find what is called the **Northwest Passage,** a route through the Arctic Ocean from the Atlantic to the Pacific; none succeeded. Today ice-breaking ships travel ahead of trade ships sailing on the Arctic Ocean, making a path through the ice.

# IN HOT WATER

Oceans aren't just fun for sailing on or swimming in, they work hard regulating the planet's temperature. Within the oceans are vast **currents** of warm and cold water (a current is a movement of water). The currents determine how warm or cold ocean water is all over the world. The sun warms water in the oceans around the equator more than at the poles. Ocean currents then continually move this warm water from the equator toward the colder regions.

Warm ocean currents heat the air above them as they travel.

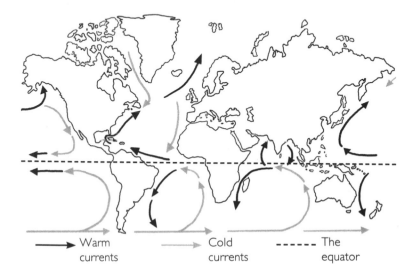

| ⟶ Warm currents | ⟶ Cold currents | - - - - The equator |

Cold ocean currents cool the air above them and move cold water away from polar regions and toward the equator. This way, the ocean balances the earth's temperature. Without currents, the warmest parts of the planet would be much hotter, and the coldest parts would be even colder.

# A JOURNEY ACROSS THE OCEAN FLOOR

Below the surface of the ocean there are mountains, hills, and valleys, just as there are on land. If you were to take a trip across the ocean floor, you would discover some interesting deep-sea details along the way.

**Continental Shelf.** A continental shelf forms at the edges of continents, where the land gently slopes away underwater. The water is usually less than 425 feet (130 m) deep along a continental shelf.

**Continental Slope.** The land slopes more steeply toward the ocean floor at the edge of a continental shelf.

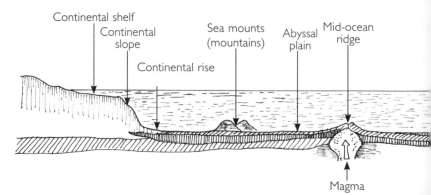

Continental shelf
Continental slope
Continental rise
Sea mounts (mountains)
Abyssal plain
Mid-ocean ridge
Magma

**Continental Rise.** A continental rise is a gentle hill formed by sediment like sand and rocks that build up at the foot of a continental slope, leading to the deep ocean.

**Abyssal Plains.** Continuously covered in thick sediment, the abyssal plains are the flattest areas on Earth and form most of the ocean's floor. They may be as much as 16,000 feet (5,000 m) from the surface of the ocean.

**Sea Mounts.** These tall, solitary mountains rise at least 3,300 feet (1,000 m) from the seafloor.

**Mid-Ocean Ridges.** Across the ocean floor, long ranges of underwater mountains form an almost continuous chain around the world. When two tectonic plates move apart underwater, magma erupts as lava to build these underwater mountains.

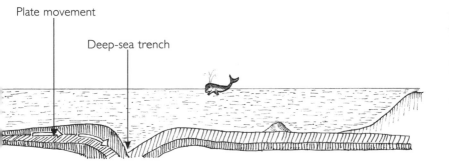

Plate movement

Deep-sea trench

**Deep-Sea Trench.** The deepest points of an ocean floor can be more than 36,000 feet (11,000 m) below the surface. The deepest trench of them all is the Mariana Trench in the Pacific Ocean.

## Under Pressure

Scientists are eager to discover more about the ocean floor, but exploring the deep ocean can be even more dangerous than going into space. As you dive underwater, the weight of the water above you increases the **pressure.** At great depths the pressure is so great that you would be crushed to death unless you were in a specially adapted submarine.

That's not all. In the lower zones of the ocean, it is pitch black and very cold, because the sun's rays can't travel that far. There are pockets of very high temperatures, too, caused by holes in the ocean floor called **hydrothermal vents,** which spew out hot liquids and gases.

# DWELLERS OF THE DEEP

The ocean provides a variety of habitats for ocean creatures and plants, and life in the ocean is incredibly diverse. It ranges from microscopic bacteria to the largest mammal on earth—the enormous blue whale, which can grow to 110 feet (34 m) in length. Some of the ocean's animals are migratory, traveling huge distances from where they mate or have their babies to feeding grounds, while other critters stay in the same place on the ocean floor their entire lives. Some burrow beneath the sand, while others swim near the surface. Scientists believe that there may be as many as 10 million species of plants and animals in the ocean that no one has ever seen, much less named.

Most of the diverse marine life lives in the top layer of the ocean, within the reach of sunlight but where the ocean temperatures are relatively cool.

## Fisheries

The oceans are an important source of food, but modern fishing methods may put this source at risk. So many fish are taken out of the ocean that not enough fish are left to spawn (release fertilized eggs to grow more fish) and grow to full size. Researchers have found that about 75 percent of the major marine fish supplies are in danger of disappearing because of overfishing. Pollution, habitat destruction, and global warming also threaten marine life. Species of fish endangered

## Is the Dead Sea Really Dead?

Depends on what you mean by "dead." Certainly it is too salty to support much marine life, though it does support swimmers who can float easily in the water.

by overfishing include: tuna, salmon, haddock, halibut, and cod—some of the most popular fish to eat. In the nineteenth century, codfish weighing up to 200 pounds (90.7 kg) were not uncommon; today a 40-pound (18.1-kg) cod is considered huge. Fish farming may one day solve this problem, but farmers must be careful to avoid pollution and overharvesting fish food.

## Coral Reefs

Thousands of animal and plant species inhabit the busy underwater communities of coral reefs. Coral looks like rocks or petrified plants, but it is actually made from the limestone skeleton of a tiny, spineless, carnivorous animal called a **coral polyp.** Coral polyps live in groups called **colonies.** Colonies grow quickly. One polyp can become a colony of 25,000 polyps in just three years. Each polyp uses calcium from the water to build a case of limestone around itself like a house, with a floor and walls. Polyps cannot move from their limestone homes, and their cases remain after the polyps die. Each case forms a foundation for another polyp to build a house on, and as the cases build up and out, the formation is called a **coral reef.**

The **Great Barrier Reef** off the coast of Australia is so big that it can be seen from space, making it the largest structure created by any group of animals. These tiny builders have existed on the earth for more than 200 million years. They grow in clear, fairly shallow warm water (64° to 91°F / 18° to 33°C). Coral cannot grow in polluted water or in water carrying soil from the land, such as at the mouths of rivers.

Coral reefs are mostly found in shallow tropical water and are among the world's most endangered ecosystems.

# LIFE ON THE OCEAN FLOOR

Most of the fisheries and marine ecosystems are near the water surface, dependent on solar energy to support the plants and microscopic organisms that help life flourish in the ocean. But solar energy can reach only so deep into ocean waters, and photosynthesis (the sun-dependent process organisms use to grow) cannot occur below 660 feet (200 m). This lack of energy, along with the sinking of cold, subpolar water, makes most of the deep ocean floor a frigid environment with few life forms. However, geothermal hot springs do exist along the centers of mid-ocean ridges, sending dissolved minerals and heat into the water, allowing specially adapted bacteria to survive. These bacteria are the bottom of a food chain that supports a surprising diversity of marine life, including giant tubeworms, clams, and mussels. These miraculous animals don't mind the water pressure of up to 65 pounds per square foot (0.03 kg per $cm^2$)—but humans would be crushed to death at that pressure.

Animals that can survive with no sunlight, at extreme temperatures, and despite bone-crushing pressures help scientists to understand the planet better. And the fact that creatures have adapted to these extreme conditions makes some scientists believe that there may be life on other planets in the universe, or even in our own solar system.

# WHERE IN THE WORLD ARE YOU?

# THE MARVEL OF MAPS

Not so long ago, travelers needed maps to figure out how to get from one place to another. Without maps, hikers couldn't find their way out of the woods, pirates couldn't find buried treasure, and vacationers couldn't find their hotels. Today Global Positioning Satellites (**GPS**) and the Internet make traveling easier, but that doesn't mean that maps are old-fashioned.

A map is a two-dimensional picture of the world. It shows you a bird's-eye view of places. There are many different types of maps—from street maps, to **topographical maps,** to survey maps. Every type of map tells you something different about a place. Some, like topographical maps, show physical features such as mountains and rivers. Others show concepts—things that our human minds have figured out—like political boundaries, names of places, or even climate zones; these are things that satellite images can't show.

Maps are also useful when comparing places. It is easy to see that Asia is the largest continent or that the tip of South America is close to Antarctica when you look at a world map. Maps often include a **scale** that tells you how to figure out distance on that particular map. They often contain a **legend** that explains the symbols used on a map. For example, the capital city might be marked with a star and other cities marked with a dot. Or blue lines might indicate rivers and black lines might indicate roads.

Maps use points, lines, and shapes to tell you what you need to know. Points usually show where a specific place is located. Depending on the map, that place can be a city or a special landmark, such as a mountain peak (or a buried treasure). Lines represent borders, roads, and rivers (or the path to a buried treasure). What the shaded areas mean usually depends on the map. A map of rivers might have watersheds shaded in. A climate map might use different colors to indicate different climate zones. A historical map might use shaded areas to show where things used to be.

# READING MAPS

The four main points of a **compass,** the device used to determine direction, are **n**orth, **e**ast, **s**outh, and **w**est. Remember them easily with this saying: **N**ever **E**at **S**hredded **W**heat. The initial letter of each word reminds you of the order of the compass directions clockwise from the top. North is always at the top of the map.

Lines of **longitude** (from the North Pole to the South Pole) and **latitude** (parallel to the equator) divide maps and globes into a kind of grid. These divisions come to us from Ptolemy (c. 100–170), the world's first geographer. Longitude and latitude give us a reasonably easy, precise, and universal way of pinpointing any specific location on Earth, especially in the ocean, where landmarks are scarce.

## Why Is North Always at the Top of Maps?

In the early days of mapmaking, north was not always at the top. It used to be that Jerusalem, a holy site in many religions, often was set at the top of maps. But once globes became popular during the period of European cultural development called the Renaissance, it seemed logical to mapmakers to put north at the top of maps, for easy viewing of the "important" landmass they called home—Europe.

If you drew an imaginary line on the earth's surface exactly the same distance from the North Pole and South Pole, you would have drawn the equator. It's the line that divides the earth into a Northern Hemisphere and a Southern Hemisphere at the earth's widest point. And, it is the place where the sun passes directly overhead at noon on March 21, the spring equinox, and at noon on September 21, the fall equinox. Most of the landmasses are in the Northern Hemisphere.

The equator lies at 0° latitude. The equator was an obvious place to call ground zero because it is based on the sun's position. But where on earth to call 0° of longitude? Mapmakers puzzled, and various solutions were proposed, mainly using a country's capital as zero degrees for maps made in that country. But in 1884, when Great Britain was a superpower, the International Meridian Conference adopted the Greenwich meridian as the universal **prime meridian,** or 0° longitude. The Greenwich meridian runs through the Royal Observatory in England.

# HOW GPS WORKS

GPS stands for Global Positioning System. Dreamed up by the U.S. military, the system is made up of 24 satellites that orbit the earth about 12,000 miles above us, transmitting data about their location and the current time to a GPS receiver. Using solar power as fuel and traveling at about 7,000 miles (11,265 km) per hour, they each orbit the earth about every 12 hours.

Here's how GPS works: A satellite tracks your vehicle's location or the location of your handheld GPS device and, based

on maps that have been loaded via CD into the GPS unit, the device guides you using visual and voice prompts to whatever address you've selected—be it a small town, an airport, or a specific street address.

## High-Tech Hide and Seek

Most GPS devices are sold with cars, and kids can't drive. But you don't have to drive to get involved with **geocaching,** a worldwide, high-tech hide-and-seek activity. Participants use a GPS receiver or other navigational techniques to hide and find containers called "geocaches" on all seven continents (even Antarctica!).

Generally, geocaching begins with registering on a Web site. A typical geocache is a small waterproof container with a book inside. The geocacher uses coordinates from the Web site to search for the cache, enters the date found into the logbook, and signs it with an established code name. The containers also may contain items for trading, usually toys or souvenirs of little value. If you take something out, you are expected to leave something behind for the next person to find.

# CONTINENTALLY SPEAKING

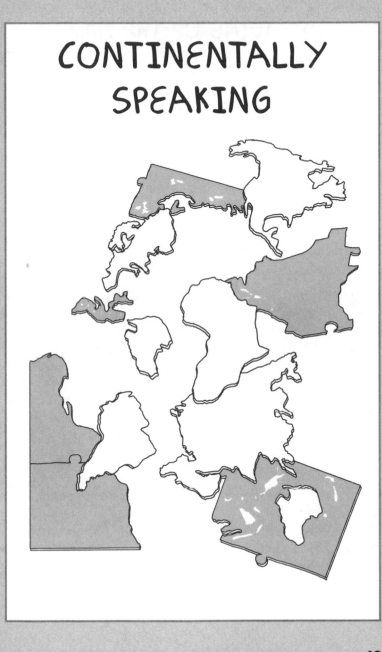

# DIVIDING UP THE MAP

The earth's large pieces of land are called continents. **Asia** is the largest continent, followed by **Africa, North America, South America, Antarctica, Europe,** and **Australia.** Some geographers group Australia and many of the Pacific Islands, including New Zealand, into a continent they call **Australia/ Oceania.**

Continents, with the exception of Antarctica, are divided into different countries. Some borders between the countries are based on natural land features, such as rivers or lakes. For example, the Rio Grande (*rio* means river in Spanish) forms part of the border between Mexico and the southern United States.

Sometimes borders between countries change because of war. In 2005, for example, southern Sudan became a semi-autonomous region within the country of Sudan after years of civil war. A January 2011 popular vote held in the region split Sudan into two countries, and the Republic of South Sudan became the newest country on the world map in July. A peaceful separation happened in 1991 when the USSR (Union of Soviet Socialist Republics) broke apart to form 15 different countries—Armenia, Azerbaijan, Belarus, Estonia, Georgia, Kazakhstan, Kyrgyzstan, Latvia, Lithuania, Moldova, Russia, Tajikistan, Turkmenistan, Ukraine, and Uzbekistan.

Sometimes countries change their names. When resource-hungry European powers started exploring Africa in the 1800s, armies were sent into Africa to unify different tribes into colonies under European rule. When those African colonies gained their independence in the 1900s, they some-times chose new names. For example, French Sudan became Mali and German Southwest Africa became Namibia.

# ENORMOUS ASIA

The largest continent on Earth, Asia accounts for 30 percent of the world's land area and contains **Russia,** the world's largest country. With a population of 4 billion, Asia is home to 60 percent of the world's population and includes three of the four most populous countries—**China, India,** and **Indonesia.** Asia is the only continent that borders two other continents: Africa and Europe. In the winter when ice forms in the Bering Sea, it sometimes joins with a third continent: North America.

## What Else Is Special about Asia?

Asia has more going for it than just its size. Here are more fun facts about this continent.

• The equator passes through Indonesia, a nation of 17,508 islands. The rest of Asia is north of the equator.

• The northern reaches of Asia lie within the Arctic Circle. This region is part of Russia and is called **Siberia.** Siberia is sparsely populated because the climate is so harsh. Eastern Siberia has winter temperatures as low as −94°F (−70°C). Siberia is rich with mineral resources, but it is most famous for its prison system, including the labor camps where Russians were sent for political crimes in the twentieth century.

• China is the most populous country in Asia. It is both an ancient civilization—with roots that can be traced back 8,000 to 10,000 years—and a modern nation that was created in 1949 as the People's Republic of China. China's huge population makes it important to the rest of the world. All those people need jobs, and Chinese manufacturing supplies many of the things people in other countries want to buy. But China buys things, too—such as the fossil fuels needed (including oil) to power those factories. As the country becomes wealthier, more people buy consumer goods made in other countries, such as refrigerators, computers, televisions, and designer clothes.

• India is the second most populous country in Asia. Its large population, like that of China, provides many goods and services important to the rest of the world, buys imported goods, and uses resources from its own country and around the world.

• The Asian country of Japan sits where the Pacific, Philippine, and Eurasian tectonic plates meet (see page 26). Earthquakes are frequent in Japan, and occasionally they do serious damage, as in 2011 when an earthquake just off the coast caused a tsunami that killed an estimated 25,000 people.

• The mountains of Japan include about 200 active volcanoes. That means that 10 percent of the world's most active volcanoes are located in this one country! **Mount Fuji** is Japan's tallest and most famous mountain, with an elevation of 12,388 feet (3,776 m); it is a dormant (sleeping but not extinct) volcano that last erupted in 1707.

• **Tokyo,** the capital city of Japan and a major economic and political center, is the world's largest city. It has an estimated population of 35.1 million people.

• **Seoul,** South Korea, is the second largest city in the world with an estimated population of 20.6 million people.

• The **Himalayas,** the highest mountain range in the world, stretch about 1,860 miles (3,000 km) across Asia, running through six countries: Bhutan, Tibet, India, Nepal, Pakistan, and Afghanistan.

• **Mount Everest** is the tallest mountain in the world with an elevation of 29,035 feet (8,850 m). It is located in Nepal.

• Three mighty rivers—the **Indus, Brahmaputra,** and **Yangtze**—originate, or start, in the Himalayas.

• **Hong Kong** is an island off the coast of China. It is one of the most densely populated places in the world and has more skyscrapers than any other city. There are more people who live or work above the fourteenth floor of the many buildings in Hong Kong than anywhere else on earth.

• The **Arabian Peninsula,** on the western edge of Asia, is the largest peninsula (a piece of land surrounded on three sides by water) in the world.

• The **Middle East** is part of Asia. It is made up of the countries of the Arabian Peninsula and those that border the Persian Gulf. The Persian Gulf is an extension of the Indian Ocean located between Iran and the Arabian Peninsula. The Middle East includes the countries of Syria, Jordan, Lebanon, Israel, Saudi Arabia, Yemen, Oman, United Arab Emirates (U.A.E.), Qatar, Bahrain, Kuwait, Iraq, and Iran.

• Many countries in the Middle East have large quantities of crude oil underground and available for drilling. The oil is used to made gasoline to fuel cars and heating oil to warm buildings.

• Cherrapunji, India, may be the wettest place on Earth. Between August 1860 and July 1861, a record of 905 inches (2,299 cm) of rain fell.

• The country of **Qatar** in the Arabian Peninsula is the wealthiest nation in the world.

• Asia is the only continent where tigers and giant pandas are found in the wild.

• Russia is so big that it stretches across 11 time zones. Its two largest cities, **Moscow,** the capital, and **St. Petersburg,** are both located on the western (European) side of the country but most of its land is located on the eastern (Asian) side.

# FRACTURED AFRICA

The second largest continent, Africa accounts for about 20 percent of the Earth's landmass. Surrounded by water on all sides, Africa was once connected to Asia in its northeast

corner by the Sinai Peninsula, where the Suez Canal now joins the Red Sea and the Mediterranean Sea.

Why is it a "fractured" continent? Because when the African and Arabian tectonic plates (see page 26) separated about 35 million years ago, a huge fault line was created in Africa. That fault line is the **Great Rift Valley.** In a few million years, the eastern part of Africa—the eastern portion beyond the Great Rift Valley—will probably split off from the African plate and form a new plate. The sea will invade the gap created by the separation and form a new ocean basin. And that means Africa will become two continents—or one continent and one big island.

With all this tectonic plate action, it is not surprising that the Great Rift Valley is home to 30 active and semi-active volcanoes and countless hot springs. Volcanic eruptions are responsible for the landscape along the length of the rift—perpendicular cliffs, mountain ridges, rugged valleys, and a series of about 30 very deep lakes along its entire length, including **Lake Tanganyika,** the second deepest lake in the world.

## What Else Is Special about Africa?

Africa isn't just interesting for its moving and shaking. Here are more things to know about this continent.

• Africa has a population of 922 million people, which makes it the second most populous continent.

• **Nigeria** is Africa's most-populous nation. With 146 million people, it is the eighth most populous nation in the world.

• The people of Africa are divided into several thousand different ethnic groups, which speak an estimated two thousand different languages.

• The world's longest river is the **Nile.** It runs through the African countries of Burundi, Democratic Republic of Congo, Egypt, Ethiopia, Rwanda, South Sudan, Sudan, Tanzania, and Uganda.

• The world's largest hot desert is the **Sahara** in northern Africa. It is part of the landscape of the African countries of Algeria, Chad, Egypt, Libya, Mali, Mauritania, Morocco, Niger, Sudan, Tunisia, and Western Sahara.

• **Mount Kilimanjaro** is the highest mountain in Africa, with an elevation of 19,340 feet (5,895 m). It is snowcapped all year even though it is only 230 miles (370 km) miles from the equator!

• The equator runs through Africa, making it the most tropical of all the continents.

• **Madagascar** is the largest island off the coast of Africa. About 75 percent of the species found in Madagascar live nowhere else on Earth. This includes dozens of species of lemurs and chameleons—and even giant hissing cockroaches.

• Most of the world's gold and diamonds come from Africa, which is also rich in other natural resources, such as minerals.

• Around 60,000 B.C., early man left Africa and settled in India and Australia, and then West Asia, Europe, and China.

# RESOURCE-RICH NORTH AMERICA

The third largest continent, North America stretches south from the Arctic Circle, through the country of Panama, and to the northern tip of South America, just 500 miles (800 km) north of the equator. North America includes an area called Central America. The islands of the Caribbean are also part of North America. (To view Central America see the maps on pages 72 and 75.)

Water and other natural resources are abundant in most of the continent. The sheer variety of environments—arctic tundra, grasslands, temperate forest, desert, and rain forest— means an incredible variety of plants and animals, too.

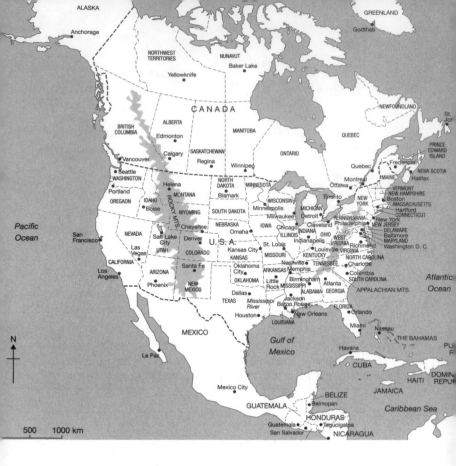

## What Else Is Special about North America?

Natural resources are just part of this continent's big picture. Here are additional facts about North America.

• North America is surrounded on three sides by ocean—the Arctic, Atlantic, and Pacific oceans.

• North America includes many islands, including **Greenland,** the world's largest island.

• The **Caribbean Sea** has the greatest concentration of islands in North America—about 7,000.

• The island nations of the Caribbean are sometimes called the **West Indies** because that's what the explorer Christopher Columbus (1451–1506) thought he had found when he landed there.

• The largest country in North America is **Canada.** It is the second largest country in the world. The **United States of America** is the third largest country in the world.

• The largest city in North America is **Mexico City,** the capital of the country of Mexico. It has a population of 20.4 million people. It is ranked as the third largest city in the world. New York City comes in fourth with an estimated population of 19.8 million people.

• **New York City,** a city of immigrants, is the most diverse city in the world, with 800 different languages spoken.

• The **San Andreas Fault** runs through the state of California. The fault is a boundary line between two tectonic plates: the Pacific plate and the North American plate (see page 26). All the land west of the fault on the Pacific plate is moving slowly to the northwest, and all the land east of the fault is moving southwest at a rate of about 1⅓ to 1½ inches (3.4 to 3.8 cm) each year. Earthquakes are frequent along the fault.

• **Mount McKinley,** also called Mount Denali, is located in Alaska. It is the highest peak in North America at 20,324 feet (6,194 m). **Mount Kea** in Hawaii would be taller, but much of its height is below water, which doesn't count toward its elevation.

• The most reported tornadoes happen in the United States, where there are around 1,000 per year. The majority of them take place in what is known as **Tornado Alley**—in the states of Nebraska, Kansas, Oklahoma, and Texas. Texas alone has an average of 125 tornadoes a year!

• Most of **Central America** rests on the small but geologically active **Caribbean plate** (see page 26), accounting for the region's numerous deadly earthquakes and volcanoes.

• The **Isthmus of Panama** connects North America to South America. An isthmus is a narrow strip of land with water on both sides that connects two large land areas.

• Parts of the Arctic Circle are covered by a permanent ice cap. Greenland and far northern Canada have an arctic climate, which is better for polar bears than humans so the farther north you go, the smaller the population.

• The lowest point in North America is **Death Valley,** California, at 282 feet (86 m) below sea level.

• **Lake Superior,** on the border between the United States and Canada, is North America's largest freshwater lake. It covers 31,700 square miles (82,100 km$^2$).

• The first human inhabitants of North America crossed over to Alaska on a land bridge from northeastern Asia roughly 20,000 years ago and then moved southward.

• North America is important to the rest of the world because it produces the greatest amount of the world's corn, meat, cotton, soybeans, tobacco, and wheat, along with a variety of other food.

# LONG AND LEAN SOUTH AMERICA

At 6.9 million square miles (17.9 million km$^2$), South America ranks as the fourth largest continent, but much of the land—rugged mountains and inaccessible rain forest—is virtually uninhabited by humans. This long, narrow continent runs from the equator nearly to the South Pole. The northern part of

South America, near the equator, is generally hot and wet. In the southern part, near the South Pole, it can be very cold.

Three centuries of **European colonization** shows in the cultures of South America. Roman Catholicism, introduced by Spain, is the majority religion of the region. Spanish and Portuguese (in Brazil, the largest country) are the dominant languages. The biggest impact the Europeans had on the continent was the spreading of many diseases, which quickly sickened the native population. Shortly after the first European contact with the **New World,** as explorers called North and South America, about 80 percent of the native population died of smallpox, diphtheria, measles, mumps, typhus, and other **Old World** diseases.

## What Else Is Special about South America?

From mountain peaks to crashing surf, South America claims some unique geographic features. Here are extra facts about this continent.

• The **Andes Mountains** run all the way down the west coast of South America. It is very cold on the peaks of these high mountains, even in the warm north of the continent.

• From its main source in the Andes, near the equator, the **Amazon River** runs east to the Atlantic Ocean. The Amazon isn't the longest river in the world, but it does send the largest volume of water into the ocean of any river in the world.

• Grassland south of the Amazon rain forest is known as **pampas.** The **Atacama Desert,** which is mostly uninhabited, is found along the southern west coast of South America, between the Andes Mountains and the Pacific Ocean.

• The vast majority of South Americans live in cities. The largest South American country in both size and population is **Brazil,** which is the fifth largest country in the world. The largest city in South America is **São Paulo,** Brazil.

• The harbor at **Rio de Janeiro** on Guanabara Bay in the Atlantic Ocean is considered one of the natural wonders of the world. The bay creates a huge natural harbor protected by two tall mountains that stand guard at the mouth of the bay: Sugar Loaf Mountain and Corcovodo Mountain. Sugar Loaf Mountain got its name because its bare ground and lopsided shape makes it look like a "loaf" of sugar, which is how sugar used to be sold. Corcovado means "hunchback" in Portuguese, and the mountain has a humped shape. On top of Corcovado is the statue of Christ the Redeemer, one of the seven wonders of the modern world.

• The **Amazon River basin** is the world's largest tropical rain forest, at 2.5 million square miles—which is just about the same size as the continental United States (that means without Hawaii and Alaska). The rain forest covers about one-third of the South American continent.

• The **Galápagos Islands,** off the coast of the country of Ecuador, are famous as the place that led scientist **Charles Darwin** (1809–1882) to develop his famous theory of evolution. Residents of the Galápagos include **finches, tortoises, penguins, albatrosses,** and the **blue-footed booby.**

• The world's southernmost city is **Puerto Toro,** Chile.

• South America is important to the rest of the world because it has abundant natural resources, grows an important share of the world's food supply, and is a growing presence on the global economic stage.

# FROZEN ANTARCTICA

Antarctica is the most extreme location on the planet. This frozen land of snow and rock is the coldest, windiest, driest, loneliest, and least hospitable landmass. It's the planet's southernmost continent and does not belong to any one country—at least for now. In the past various countries have tried to claim ownership of the land, but an international treaty now governs Antarctica. Today only a few thousand scientists live and work there.

Including its permanent sheet of ice, Antarctica has an area of about 5.5 million square miles (14.3 million km$^2$), which makes it the fifth largest continent. It is the most isolated continent on Earth, and you'd have to sail a distance of 600 miles (1,000 km) to reach the southernmost tip of South America, its nearest neighbor.

## What Else Is Special about Antarctica?

If learning about extreme Antarctica makes you want to read on, you're in luck. Here are even more facts about this wild continent.

• Surrounded by the Southern Ocean, Antarctica is an ice-locked landmass located at the South Pole.

• The average annual temperature inland is −70°F (−57°C). The lowest temperature ever recorded on Earth was in the Antarctic, an incredible −128.5°F (−89°C).

• Underneath its ice cap, the eastern part of Antarctica is rock, mostly above sea level.

• West Antarctica was formed by volcanic action. Under the weight of its ice, much of the land, which seems to be a group of islands held together by permanent ice, is actually below sea level.

• Probably the best-known volcano on Antarctica is **Mount Erebus,** which is part of the Pacific Ring of Fire. With a summit elevation of 12,448 feet (3,794 m), it looms over McMurdo Station, an American research base on Ross Island.

• Antarctica is technically a **frozen desert.** It is thought that in some spots, such as McMurdo Sound, rain or snow hasn't fallen for more than two million years!

## New Year's Moving Day

If someone could insert a rod through the entire planet to show how the earth rotates, it would go through the North and South poles. In the Arctic the rod would have to be inserted into the sea-bed of the Arctic Ocean. In Antarctica the South Pole lies inland. Norwegian polar explorer Roald Amundsen (1872–1928) and his team of adventurers planted the first flag on the South Pole, and today the geographic South Pole is the site of the Amundsen-Scott Station, a United States scientific base. But the exact place where the South Pole is located moves every year because it is on an ice sheet that migrates about 33 feet (10 m) annually. So the pole that marks the spot is ceremoniously moved every New Year's Day.

But don't confuse the *geographic* South Pole (0° longitude) with the *magnetic* South Pole. That's about 1,700 miles (2,740 km) away!

• With the exception of a few bare peaks and "dry" valleys, almost all this land is covered by an immense **ice sheet** an average of 1 mile (1.6 km) thick. Its greatest known thickness is about 3 miles (4.8 km)—that's 15,670 feet (4,776 m).

• Because the snow on Antarctica never melts, it never goes away—ever. So it builds up, and up. The average elevation of Antarctica is about 7,500 feet (2,286 m), which makes it the highest continent on Earth.

• The high elevation of Antarctica explains why it is colder at the South Pole than the North Pole. The North Pole is at sea level, an elevation of zero, and the South Pole is at 9,300 feet (2.9 m); air is cooler at higher elevations.

• The annual snowfall in the interior of the continent is only 1 to 2 inches (2.5 to 5 cm), although more snow falls along the coast and on the windward side (the side the wind is blowing) of coastal mountains—10 to 20 inches (25 to 51 cm) per year.

## All about Icebergs

When a big chunk of ice breaks off from a glacier, the process is called **calving**. Generally 10,000 to 15,000 icebergs are calved each year. Chunks of ice smaller than an iceberg are called bergy bits and growlers.

Icebergs are larger than they appear, since only 10 to 15 percent can be seen above the surface of the water. To be classified as an iceberg, the ice must be at least 16 feet (5 m) tall, 98 to 164 feet (30 to 50 m) wide, and the ice must cover an area of at least 5,382 square feet (500 m²). The largest iceberg ever measured was 208 miles (335 km) long and 60 miles (97 km) wide. Scientists estimated that if that iceberg melted and the water were captured, it would provide enough freshwater to supply London, England, for 700 years.

• The ice that covers the Antarctic holds 70 to 90 percent of the earth's freshwater reserves. Along the coast, the ice sometimes forms enormous floating sheets called **ice shelves.** The largest are the Ross Ice Shelf, the Ronne Ice Shelf, the Larsen Ice Shelf, and the Filchner Ice Shelf.

• The ice shelves are fed, in part, by huge **freshwater glaciers** moving down mountain valleys to the coasts. Glaciers also flow directly into the sea like long floating tongues; these are called glacier tongues or iceberg tongues.

• The **Lambert Glacier** on the eastern half of the continent is 25 miles (40 km) wide and more than 248 miles (400 km) long, making it the largest glacier on earth.

• Each summer tons of icebergs break off the edges of the ice shelves and float north. Sea ice—frozen seawater that forms during the winter—also breaks up during the summer, creating freely floating ice known as **pack ice.**

# WELL-SETTLED EUROPE

When you look at a world map you might wonder why Europe is considered a continent. After all, it is physically attached to Asia. Some geographers call Europe a peninsula, part of "Eurasia." But the two areas are culturally distinct— even if a few countries (such as Russia) fall within both Europe *and* Asia. So we consider Europe a continent, separated from Asia by the Ural and Caucasus mountains.

Covering 3.9 million square miles (10.1 million km$^2$), Europe is the second smallest of the continents and has been fully settled for centuries. With a total population of 731 million, it comes second only to Asia in terms of population density. Europe's agriculture and industry also are well developed. It was once covered with temperate forests, but little of that remains. The land has been grazed and farmed for centuries. Few areas of untouched wilderness are left, except in Scandinavia and northern Russia.

## What Else Is Special about Europe?

When it comes to settling down, Europe is king! Here are some fabulous facts about this continent.

• Most of Europe lies within 300 miles (483 km) of a seacoast.

• There are no deserts in Europe.

• **Vatican City,** which is located within the city of Rome, Italy, is the world's smallest country in terms of population (829). And most of the people are not even permanent residents. Covering an area of just 0.17 square miles (0.44 km$^2$), Vatican City is the world's smallest country by area as well. It serves as the residence of the pope, the head of the Catholic Church.

• Besides Vatican City, there are other tiny nations in Europe. **San Marino,** located within the borders of Italy, is the oldest

surviving sovereign state and constitutional republic in the world. It was founded on September 3, 301. Densely populated, **Monaco** is a city state on the Côte d' Azur, bordered on three sides by its neighbor France. Monaco is famous for its casinos, tourism, and beautiful location on the French Riviera. The small, landlocked nation of **Liechtenstein** has the highest Gross Domestic Product (GDP) per person in the world.

• The island country of **Iceland** is basically one big volcano, formed over millions of years as molten rock bubbled up from the sea floor. Other features of Iceland include glaciers, lava wastes, ice caps, and boiling lakes.

## World's Happiest Continent

According to a study conducted in 2005, Iceland, Sweden, Denmark, and the Netherlands topped the list of countries where the people rated themselves as happy with their lives. Three other European countries made the top 10 list: Ireland, Switzerland, and the United Kingdom. (The United States came in at number 13.)

• The mountains in northern Norway are home to the largest glacier on mainland Europe, **Jostedal Glacier.**

• Norway is famous for its **fjords** (pronounced fee-yords). A fjord is a narrow, steep-sided inlet to the sea carved by glaciers.

• Lapland, in northern Norway, and parts of Sweden and Finland lie within the Arctic Circle.

• The Netherlands is a whole country with an elevation that is basically below sea level. Since the Middle Ages, the Dutch have built dikes (large barriers of earth and stone) to hold back water and reclaim land from the sea. These reclaimed lands, called **polders,** once were drained and kept dry by power generated bywindmills. Today other sources of power run the pumps that keep the polders dry.

• The **Alps** are a mountain range dividing southern Europe from northern Europe. The **Ural** and **Caucasus** mountains form a border with Asia.

• Italy has Europe's only active volcanoes: **Mount Etna** (on the island of Sicily) and **Mount Vesuvius.**

• **Russia, Turkey, Georgia,** and **Kazakhstan** are all countries that are partly in Europe and partly in Asia.

• Europe is important to the rest of the world because the European Union (EU) represents the largest and most diverse economy of the world. The member nations of the EU are able to keep their own identities, cultures, laws, and governments but cooperate with the other nations when it comes to trade and financial matters. They share the same currency, called the euro. Europe is also the world's biggest contributor of money to help developing countries.

# DOWN UNDER
# AUSTRALIA/OCEANIA

Is Australia a country, an island, or a continent? Most geographers these days consider the *country* of Australia to be part of a larger *continent* that includes New Zealand and thousands of Pacific islands and coral atolls, or reefs that surround lagoons. Some say the most accurate name is Australia/Oceania; others call it Australasia. Australia/Oceania is located in the Southern Hemisphere, southeast of Asia, and surrounded by the Indian and Pacific oceans. It is the smallest continent in terms of size and the second smallest in population. It may be "small" in terms of dry land; however, it is spread over 3.3 million square miles (8.5 million km$^2$) of ocean.

## What Else Is Special about the Land Down Under?

Although Australia/Oceania does not have a lot of land, it can boast about many other things. Here are just a few of this continent's important facts.

• The largest country in Australia/Oceania is Australia. Australia is the driest inhabited continent, the flattest, and has the least fertile soils.

• There are more sheep in Australia/Oceania than people.

- About 70 percent of all Australians live in a city.

- **Aborigines**, the indigenous people of Australia, traditionally live in the dry and dusty **Outback** in the center of Australia.

- Australia has the greatest number of reptiles of any country in the world, with about 755 species.

- **The Great Barrier Reef** is the largest coral reef in the world and lies a short distance off the coast of Australia. It is considered one of the wonders of the natural world, and it is home to some 1,500 species of fish, 400 types of coral, 500 species of seaweed, 16 species of sea snake, and six species of sea turtle. It is also an important breeding ground for humpback whales.

- **Tasmania** is an island off the southern coast of Australia. It is home to the fierce little Tasmanian devil as well as several other animal species that are now extinct on mainland Australia.

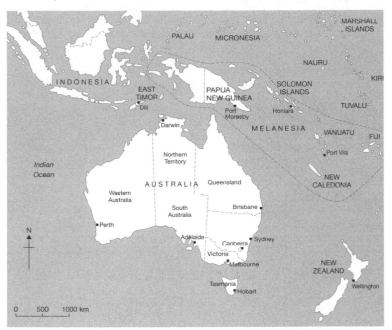

## Home, Sweet . . . Pouch?

Many marsupials, such as kangaroos, live
only in Australia. Marsupials are animals
that grow their young in external pouches
instead of inside their bodies. Other marsupials include
the platypus, koala bear, wombat, and kookaburra.

But why don't people in Europe look into the trees and see
koala bears? Conditions on Australia/Oceania led to the development of these mammals. When the continent broke away from
Antarctica about 140 million years ago, it drifted north into warm
waters, and the land became isolated from the other continents.
Unlike other areas of the world, Australia never experienced an
ice age, which means the environment remained relatively stable
over the course of 40 million years or so when other continents went through major periods of animal extinctions. And
so Australia is home to the koala bear—and to the kangaroo.
In fact, more than 80 percent of the country's flowering plants,
mammals, reptiles, and frogs live only in Australia. And most of
Australia's freshwater fish and almost half of its birds can only be
found on this one special place on earth, too.

• **New Zealand, Papua New Guinea** (considered part of
Asia), and the **Solomon Islands** are part of the Pacific Ring
of Fire (see page 30).

• New Zealanders are called **Kiwis**, an affectionate term that
refers to the flightless kiwi bird—and not the fruit with the
brown, fuzzy skin.

• Earthquakes and volcanoes are common on New Zealand
because the land is split between the Australian plate and the
Pacific plate. When New Zealand separated from Australia

about 100 million years ago, mammals were just emerging. Because of this timing, New Zealand had few mammals until humans spread across the globe about 80 million years later. There were, however, plenty of flightless—and wingless—birds.

• Australia is home to the greatest number of **marsupial species**, such as koalas and kangaroos, in the world. Marsupial moms usually carry their babies in a pouch as the babies grow.

• Many of the **Pacific Islands** are **volcanic islands** that rose from the sea floor through hot spots in the Pacific Ocean

## Where in the World Are the Seven Wonders?

In the fifth century B.C., a historian by the name of Herodotus sat down and wrote a list of the seven wonders of the world. People have been arguing over the list ever since—what he included, what he didn't include. The list itself didn't survive, but scholars think the seven wonders of the ancient world included:

• Great Pyramid of Giza
• Hanging Gardens of Babylon
• Statue of Zeus at Olympia
• Temple of Artemis at Ephesus
• Mausoleum of Maussollos at Halicarnassus
• Colossus of Rhodes
• Lighthouse of Alexandria

Don't be surprised if you've never heard of all these wonders— or visited any of them. Most of them are long gone. Some historians don't think the hanging gardens ever existed. The only wonder you can still visit is the Great Pyramid of Giza, which is located in Egypt.

Basin. Most of these volcanic islands, such as **Fiji** and the **Solomon Islands,** are very small and have tall mountain ranges.

• About 15 million people live on the islands of Australia/Oceania.

• Australia/Oceania is important to the rest of the world as a vacation spot. The country of Australia, and the continent to a lesser extent, is rich in mineral resources, including coal, diamonds, gold, iron ore, natural gas, nickel, petroleum, and uranium.

# ISLAND HOPPING

# THE WORLD'S BIGGEST ISLAND

A tropical island paradise is a good spot for a vacation. But which one? Planet Earth has more than 100,000 islands, so there are plenty to choose from. The difference between an island and a continent is a matter of size. It seems like finding the world's biggest island would be easy as looking at a map or a globe and picking out the largest area of land that's totally surrounded by water.

Well, it's not that simple. You could be fooled into thinking that the world's biggest island is Australia. After all, it is surrounded by ocean and is more than three times the size of its nearest rival, **Greenland.** However, geographers have decided that there has to be a cutoff point between islands and continents. Australia is often classed as a continent, bouncing it out of the top spot for biggest island. In this book, it is included as part of Australia/Oceania (see pages 84 to 88). This leaves Greenland as the second biggest island. It is part of the North American continent and a protectorate of the European country of Denmark, which just means that Denmark takes care of Greenland politically and financially.

## Barrier Islands

A barrier island is a long, thin, sandy piece of land parallel to the mainland coast. It makes a barrier between the mainland and raging ocean storms, protecting the coast from the full force of powerful storm waves. In the United States, barrier islands occur off the Atlantic and Gulf of Mexico coasts, where there are gently sloping sandy coastlines, as opposed to rocky coastlines. **Padre Island,** off the coast of Texas, is the longest barrier island in the world. **Assateague Island** near Maryland is a barrier island and is most famous as a home of wild ponies.

# MAKING ISLANDS

Greenland was once connected to North America, so how did it become an island? There are two types of islands: continental and oceanic. Greenland is a continental island.

**Continental Islands.** These islands are part of a continent that has been flooded so much that only the highest points lie above sea level, creating islands. Most continental islands were formed at the end of the last ice age, when the huge glaciers covering the land melted. Vast amounts of **meltwater** flowed into the oceans and made sea levels rise. Those higher sea levels flooded low-lying areas at the edges of the land. In addition to creating the island of Greenland, the meltwater created more than 3,000 islands along Norway's rugged coast in Europe. The **British Isles** off the coast of mainland Europe are also continental islands. If sea levels fell far enough, the United Kingdom would be reconnected with Europe.

**Oceanic Islands.** The earth's crust is a jigsaw puzzle of moving pieces called tectonic plates (see page 26). Oceanic islands are formed by volcanic activity along the edges of these plates on the ocean floor. Where plates move

## The World's Most Endangered Country

The Maldive Islands are the flattest country on earth. At their high-est point, they only reach an altitude of about eight feet (2.4 m) above sea level. About 1,200 islands and atolls in the Indian Ocean make up this country, anchored just north of the equator. Only 200 of the islands are inhabited, but the absolute number and identity of the islands varies because old islands are constantly becoming submerged underwater and new ones are constantly created. White sandy beaches, deep-blue lagoons, and coral reefs are part of the beauty of this nation, but a rise in sea levels threatens its survival. If sea levels continue to rise at current rates, it is expected that the islands will be uninhabitable in about 100 years.

apart from each other, the earth's crust cracks, allowing hot, melted rock known as magma, to bubble up, forming an undersea volcano. The magma cools and solidifies. Eventually, the volcano grows so high that it rises above sea level, form-ing an island. **Easter Island** in the Pacific Ocean was formed this way.

Oceanic islands are also formed where one tectonic plate slips underneath the other. As the earth's crust pushes into the mantle, it melts and turns into magma. This erupts to form a chain of islands, known as an island arc. This is how the **Aleutian Islands,** located between Russia and Alaska at the northern edge of the Pacific Ocean, were created.

Hot spots also create islands. These superheated places deep inside the earth are so hot that they can melt the earth's crust, allowing lava to burst through to form volcanoes. This lava builds over time until the volcano is tall enough to break through the surface of the sea. Surtsey island off the coast of

Iceland in the Atlantic Ocean is an example of this kind of oceanic island. It formed right in front of Icelanders' eyes in 1963!

Hot spots build islands hundreds of miles away from tectonic plate boundaries. Over millions of years, a single hot spot can build a whole chain of islands. This is because a hot spot stays put as the tectonic plate above slowly moves over it. As the plate moves, the hot spot melts new holes in the crust, creating new volcanoes and new islands.

The **Hawaiian Island chain** was created in this way. There are 132 Hawaiian islands, and the newest is being built right now at the bottom of the Pacific Ocean. But don't plan a vacation there just yet—it will take tens of thousands of years for that little lump of lava to rise above the ocean's surface.

# WE'RE NOT AN ISLAND *ATOLL*

Once a new volcanic island has drifted away from the hot spot that created it, the island starts to sink. Rain, wind, and waves wear the island away until it disappears below the surface of the ocean forever. When this

## Hurricane Capital of the World

Vacationers love the Cayman Islands, located 150 miles south of Cuba in the western Caribbean. Pristine beaches, coral reefs perfect for diving, and high-end resorts attract people from all over North America. This British territory is also the hurricane capital of the world. Grand Cayman, the largest of the three Cayman isles, is hit or affected by at least one hurricane every two years, more than any other spot in the Atlantic.

happens, that island needs a new name. For example, the oldest and most remote Hawaiian island is not an island at all. It used to be, but now it's just an **atoll**. An atoll is formed when a coral reef grows around a volcanic island. As the coral reef grows, the volcanic island is slowly destroyed and eventually all that is left is a ring of coral with shallow water or a **lagoon** in the middle.

# HOW DO MOUNTAINS CLIMB?

Planet Earth's mountain ranges are jagged towers of rock that rise high into the skies. How did they get there? Why are they all so different in size and shape? Mountains form through processes that begin deep below the surface of the earth. It takes a long time to make a mountain. Scientists have found 18,000-year-old seashells in rock samples from the Himalayan and Andes mountains—far, far away from any beach. This suggests that these mountains were once below sea level. So how do you go from ocean floor to top of the world?

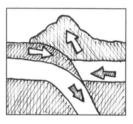

**Folds.** Mountains form when two continental tectonic plates (see page 26) crash into one another, causing the crust to crumple and pushing the land up. This is the most common way for mountains to form— the Himalayas in Asia were created in this way. And that pushing? It's still happening. Scientists have evidence that the world's highest mountain, Mount Everest, is still growing and moving.

## The Most Famous Dome Mountain

**Parícutin volcano** in the Mexican state of Michoacán is one of the natural wonders of the world because it grew right before the eyes of the farmers who lived nearby. This dome-shaped mountain began as a cornfield and ended up as a mountain in just eight short years. When this volcano first erupted in 1943, it grew so fast that it measured five stories tall in one week. Over the course of its first year, it rose 1,110 feet (336 m) into the air. It continued to erupt until it went dormant in 1952, at the height of 1,390 feet (424 m).

**Eruptions.** Repeated volcanic eruptions that happen where the continental plates meet can cause molten rock and ash to spew out from inside the Earth. The ash and rock build up over time— a long, long time—to make mountains out of flatland. **Mount Fuji** in Japan and

**Mount Rainier** in Washington State are examples of this kind of mountain.

**Faults.** Sometimes when two tectonic plates push together, they crack instead of folding, and a huge chunk of rock is pushed upward to create what is known as a **block mountain**. The **Sierra Nevada Mountains** in California are examples of block mountains.

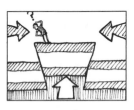

**Domes.** Dome mountains form when magma, or molten rock, in the mantle increases in pressure, pushing the earth's crust up from below. This process makes rounded, dome-shaped mountains. The **Black Hills** of South Dakota and the **Adirondack Mountains** of New York State are examples of dome mountains.

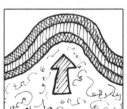

# WEAR AND TEAR

If mountains are still growing, why are some so small? Before a mountain has finished growing, wind, water, and ice set to work, wearing it down in a process called **erosion.** Erosion causes the wide variety of mountain shapes you can see today. Ice in the form of **glaciers** creates some of the most eye-catching mountain features by carving deep into the rock and bulldozing away rock and soil. In fact, glaciers in the last ice age acted like giant scouring pads, scrubbing away the tops of mountains. The older the mountains, the more wear and tear from erosion.

# THE YOUNG HIMALAYAS

The highest and largest mountain range in the world, the Himalayas stretch about 1,860 miles (3,000 km) across Asia. This mountain range contains the 15 highest peaks in the world, including Mount Everest. When the Himalayas formed, they physically separated South Asia and the Indian

## What Is a Glacier?

A glacier is a very, very big sheet of ice formed over years and years as snow falls and never melts. As the snow piles up, its weight increases and causes the snow crystals below the surface to compact into ice crystals. These ice crystals join together to form a "river" of ice that can measure 300 to 10,000 feet (91 to 3,050 m) in thickness—that's quite thick when you remember that there are 5,280 feet in a mile! Ice, as we all know, is slippery. When a glacier becomes very dense and heavy, the ice crystals deep inside it begin to slide over each other, and the glacier starts to move. Because of gravity, the movement is downward, either down a mountain or to the sea. As glaciers move, they pick up soil and rocks and deposit them elsewhere as **sediment**.

subcontinent from the rest of Asia, causing differences in climate and the development of distinctively different cultures.

Plate tectonics created this great mountain range (see page 26) about 70 million years ago—when the Indian plate collided with Eurasian plate. The Himalayas are the youngest mountains in the world, a fact that accounts in part for their great height—there hasn't been as much time for erosion to wear them down as for other, older mountains. At present they are still growing; the Indian plate pushes into the Asian continent at the rate of about $2\frac{1}{3}$ inches (6 cm) annually, slowly but surely folding and lifting up the crust of the earth as it goes.

The Himalayas play a major role in India's climate because they block the flow of cool air from the north. As a result, India's climate is very hot. The mountains also block moist air coming off the Indian Ocean from reaching Central Asia, which is why much of the interior of China is a desert region.

The Himalayas are the source of many of the world's major rivers: the Brahmaputra, Chao Phraya, Ganges, Indus, Irrawaddy, Mekong, Yangtze, and Yellow rivers (among others) start in the Himalayas. As they flow out to the sea, these rivers provide fresh water for about 3 billion people (almost half of earth's population) in Afghanistan, Bangladesh, Bhutan, China, India, Nepal, Burma, Cambodia, Tajikistan, Uzbekistan, Turkmenistan, Kazakhstan, Kyrgyzstan, Thailand, Laos, Vietnam, Malaysia, and Pakistan.

# THE OLD APPALACHIANS

The Appalachian Mountains in the United States extend from central Alabama up through the New England states and the Canadian provinces of New Brunswick, Newfoundland, and

## Mount Everest: A Natural Wonder

Mount Everest, the highest mountain in the world, is considered one of the natural wonders of the world. Every year adventurous climbers attempt to reach the top of this peak, located on the border between Nepal and Tibet. Its summit was first reached in 1953 by Sir Edmund Hillary (1919–2008) of New Zealand and Tenzing Norgay (1914–1986) of Nepal. Norgay knew the mountain as Chomolungma, the Tibetan name, which means "Mother of the Universe." However, a British surveyor-general called it Mount Everest, not knowing that the mountain had a Nepalese name. Climbing Everest has generated controversy in recent years, because nearly 200 people have died climbing the mountain.

Quebec—about 1,500 miles (2,410 km) in all. The mountains have different names in different parts of the country. They are called the Cumberland Mountains in Tennessee, the Blue Ridge Mountains in Virginia, the Alleghenies in Pennsylvania, the Adirondacks in New York, the Green Mountains in Vermont, and the White Mountains in New Hampshire. The highest point is Mount Mitchell in North Carolina at 6,684 feet (2,037 m). The oldest mountains in the world, the ancient Appalachian Mountains were formed about 300 million years ago when the tectonic plate boundaries of North America and Africa collided during the formation of Pangaea, the supercontinent (see page 28). Over the years, erosion has smoothed out the jagged peaks and knocked down the height of the mountains until they appear as mere bumps on the landscape compared to the Himalayas—or even the Rockies, located in the western region of the United States.

# A ROCKY HISTORY
# FOR THE ROCKY MOUNTAINS

The Rocky Mountains stretch from Canada down to the southwestern United States in North America. These ancient mountains formed along fault lines as the Pacific tectonic plate pushed against the North American tectonic plate. At one point, a vast ocean covered the land and deposited a lot of sand that eventually formed a **sandstone** layer in the rock. At various times the mountains were worn down by glaciers and erosion and built up again by volcanic and plate tectonic action. Like the Himalayas, the Rocky Mountains are still growing even today because the Pacific plate continues to push against North America.

The mountains form the **Continental Divide** for North America, separating the rivers that drain into the Atlantic Ocean from those that drain into the Pacific Ocean. The major rivers that flow to the Atlantic are the Arkansas, Missouri, Platte, Rio Grande, Saskatchewan, and Yellowstone rivers. Those draining to the Pacific Ocean are the Colorado, Columbia, Fraser, Snake, and Yukon rivers.

# THE LONG ANDES

This very long mountain range of rugged high peaks extends along the western part of South America, from the northern end all the way south to the islands off the southern tip of the mainland called **Tierra del Fuego** (Land of Fire). The Andes rise to a highest point of 22,835 feet (6,960 m) above sea level at the peak of **Mount Aconcagua** in Argentina.

The Andes are fold mountains, formed when Pangaea broke up and the pieces began to float away from each other (see page 28). The Pacific Ocean tectonic plate began to squeeze under the South America plate, pushing up the Andes.

The Amazon and most of the other major rivers on the South American continent originate in the Andes, which is where the continental divide for this area is located. The Andes are also home to 204 volcanoes, many of them active, including some of the planet's largest. In the far south, along the coast of Chile, large glaciers are common. And when you combine volcanoes with glaciers, you get eruptions that cause major mudslides, which can be deadly.

### Mountain Dwellers

Plants and animals that thrive on high-elevation mountains must be adapted to the cold, the lack of oxygen (air is "thinner," or holds fewer molecules as elevation increases), and the rugged landscape. The animals—like mountain goat, ibex (wild goat), sheep, mountain lion, puma, and yak—must be agile and light on their feet so they can travel easily on the steep, rocky mountain sides. Types of plants vary depending on geographic location and altitude. Lower elevations are commonly covered by forests, while very high elevations are usually treeless. Quinoa (pronounced *keen-wah*) is a grain that is specially adapted to growing in the Andes. The Incas relied on it as their staple grain—the way that traditionally people in Europe relied on wheat and people in Asia relied on rice.

Location, north or south along the mountain range (the latitude, see page 59), plays a defining role in the climates of this lengthy mountain range. In the northern region, the climate is warm and wet because those mountains are closest to the equator. Still, the high mountains are snowcapped—like **Mount Cotopaxi** in Ecuador, which is just 30 miles (48 km) from the equator. In the southern region, the mountains are relatively close to the Antarctic, and the climate is far colder.

# THE ALPS OF EUROPE

The Alps are a mountain range that curves across Europe from the Mediterranean coast, across southeastern France and northern Italy, through most of Switzerland, Austria, and Liechtenstein, and into southern Germany and Slovenia.

These fold mountains were formed 23 to 34 million years ago, when the African tectonic plate pushed toward the European tectonic plate at a rate of about 3½ inches (9 cm) a year. The shape of these mountains was greatly altered during the last ice age, when the Alps were covered by glaciers. Remnants of these glaciers can still be found at high elevations that allow mountain resorts in the Alps to offer year-round skiing. Ice Age glaciers scooped out broad valleys and formed large, deep lakes, like **Lake Geneva** and **Lake Lucerne** in Switzerland and **Lake Como** in Italy. Were it not for the bulldozing glaciers, the Alps would be closer in height to the Himalayas.

Three of the largest rivers of Europe—the **Rhine, Rhône,** and **Po**—originate in the Alps, as well as tributaries of the **Danube.**

# THE WORLD'S TALLEST MOUNTAIN PEAKS

If you wanted to climb the tallest mountain on every continent, where should you go? That's a question you could ask Jordan Romero, the youngest person ever to climb Mount Everest. He called his mom to say *hello* from the world's highest peak when he was just 13 years old! Use this table to see how the heights of the tallest mountains on each continent stack up.

| MOUNTAIN | CONTINENT | HEIGHT ABOVE SEA LEVEL |
|---|---|---|
| Everest | Asia | 29,029 feet (8,848 m) |
| Aconcagua | South America | 22,841 feet (6,962 m) |
| McKinley | North America | 20,308 feet (6,190 m) |
| Kilimanjaro | Africa | 19,340 (5,895 m) |
| Elbrus | Europe | 18,510 (5,642 m) |
| Vinson Massif | Antarctica | 16,043 (4,890 m) |
| Puncak Jaya | Australia/Oceania | 16,024 (4,884 m)* |

*Some scientists argue that Australia/Oceania's highest peak should be Mount Kosciuszco in Australia because Puncak Jaya is in Papua, New Guinea, a country that is part of the Australian continental shelf but is considered a nation of Asia. Some people who want to climb the highest mountains on each continent have ended up climbing both—just to be sure!

# WATERSHEDS, RIVERS, AND LAKES

# GOING WITH THE FLOW

Unless you are reading this book on an airplane or an ocean liner, you are probably located in the middle of a **watershed.** A watershed is the area of land where all of the water that is under it or drains off of it goes into the same place. According to the U.S. Environmental Protection Agency (EPA), there are 2,267 watersheds in the United States, including Hawaii, Alaska, and the territory of Puerto Rico.

Water falls to the ground as precipitation (such as rain or snow) and is absorbed into the soil—becoming **ground-water**—or it drains from the surface of the land into the nearest creek or stream. Streams join other streams and flow into rivers that, in turn, are fed by the groundwater through underwater springs. All of the area that drains into each creek, stream, or river is called its watershed.

If you imagine the earth as a human body, the rivers would be the veins and the arteries that carry essential supplies from place to place. Rivers provide water for drinking, cooking, washing, farming, and transportation—the big, wet roads along which people can transport themselves and their goods. Throughout history, rivers have attracted the first settlers to a new territory.

## Cradles of Civilization

A **cradle of civilization** is a place where early people are thought to have first settled down and started farming and developing cities. Asia contains two such cradles: in China along the **Yellow River** and in the Middle East, along the **Tigris-Euphrates** river system in what is now Iraq. Rivers help start civilizations because the land nearby floods frequently, which makes the soil fertile and good for farming. When people figured out how to use the rivers for irrigation (water for crops), they were able to grow a lot more food. This allowed some people to work at jobs other than farming or hunting, like making pottery and clothing, metalworking, and trade. Soon enough, whole civilizations developed.

# WHERE DO RIVERS START?

Rivers all flow downhill, thanks to gravity. A river's **source,** or starting point, is high up, sometimes on a mountain. Water from melting snow and rain trickles downward, meeting other trickles, which gather together as the water flows, until

## The Very Grand, Grand Canyon

Many people call the Grand Canyon one of the seven natural wonders of the world. It is pretty amazing because of its size, because of what it reveals about the geology and history of the area, and because of its amazing beauty.

Located in northern Arizona State, the Grand Canyon was cut by the Colorado River over centuries. The river carried away rock and more rock as it traveled to the Gulf of California in the Pacific Ocean until a deep canyon was formed. It is 277 miles (446 km) long and up to 18 miles (29 km) wide. It is more than 1 mile (1.6 km) deep at its deepest point.

If you look in the canyon, you can see many layers of rock, some that are at least two billion years old. There is evidence that the Grand Canyon was once part of a large sea, because in some layers of rock, you can find fossils of trilobites, tiny sea creatures that lived in the sea about 500 million years ago. There is also evidence of volcanic ash and lava. All of that history on view through the layers and layers of rock make the Grand Canyon a geologist's paradise.

all of those trickles form a stream. As streams flow quickly downhill, they join other streams to become rivers. Where the land flattens out away from the hills and mountains, rivers usually flow at a slower pace. The place where a river ends and flows out into a lake or ocean is called the **mouth,** and water usually picks up speed as it moves toward the mouth.

# EARTH-MOVING MACHINES

Rivers don't just move water and people—they are also the planet's very own earth-moving machines. Day and night, rivers carve out and smooth the landscape. **Canyons** and **gorges** are deep, steep-sided valleys formed by young rivers cutting mainly downward through the land. One of the largest is the **Grand Canyon** of the **Colorado River** in Arizona

State. Each year, rivers erode and transport vast quantities of sediment, or soil. When sediment builds up at the mouth of a river, it forms new land, often triangular in shape, called a **delta.** The most famous delta is that of the **Nile River** in Egypt, and it is famous because each year the river deposits a new layer of sediment, making the delta even more fertile. The **Ganges** and **Brahmaputra** rivers empty into the Bay of Bengal in the Indian Ocean, making a delta that spans most of Bangladesh and West Bengal, India; it is the world's largest delta. The **Mississippi River** makes a large delta in Louisiana State as it empties into the Gulf of Mexico.

# THE WORLD'S LONGEST RIVERS

For centuries, geographers have argued over the length of the world's rivers. You might imagine that it would be a simple process to take a measuring tape and measure from the start of a river to its finish. In reality, the length of a river is hard to calculate. This is because experts don't agree on the precise point where some rivers start or where exactly rivers finish and meet a lake or sea. As a result, the exact lengths of many rivers are hotly debated. Here's a table of the longest rivers on each continent.

| RIVER | CONTINENT | LENGTH |
|---|---|---|
| Nile | Africa | 4,159 miles (6,693 km) |
| Amazon | South America | 3,999 miles (6,436 km) |
| Yangtze | Asia | 3,915 miles (6,300 km) |
| Mississippi | North America | 3,889 miles (6,275 km) |
| Volga | Europe | 2,265 miles (3,645 km) |
| Murray | Australia/Oceania | 1,476 miles (2,375 km) |

A river delta

... ER WHERE DO I MEASURE TO?

**The Nile: The Longest River in the World**

European explorers spent much of the 1800s trying to find the source of this mysterious river that snakes its way through one of the harshest deserts in the world and into the Mediterranean Sea. Today it is often agreed that the Nile begins at Ripon Falls in the African country of Burundi. Along its meandering south to north route, two main **tributaries** (smaller streams or rivers that feed into larger bodies of water) pump water into the Nile. The White Nile travels through Burundi, Tanzania, Lake Victoria in Uganda, and South Sudan. The Blue Nile starts at Lake Tana in Ethiopia and flows into Sudan from the southeast.

The two rivers meet near the Sudanese capital of Khartoum and continue northward to Egypt. The Nile River provided the foundation for one of the oldest and richest civilizations in the world: ancient Egypt. Although you won't find any

## On the Nile with the Crocodiles

Crocodiles are probably the most famous inhabitants of the Nile River, though they also live in rivers throughout Africa. A living relic of the age of dinosaurs, crocodiles have been around for about 200 million years, snacking on fish, waterfowl, antelope, wildebeests, zebras, young elephants, and even big cats such as leopards and lions. When given the chance, they are known to prey upon domestic animals like chickens, goats, sheep, and cattle, as well as humans. Crocodiles will leave the water to hunt, if necessary, and they are surprisingly speedy on land, even though their legs are very short. A person cannot outrun an attacking crocodile.

The male crocodile usually measures 12 to 16 feet (3.5 to 5 m) long, but very old, mature crocs can grow to 18 feet (5.5 m) or more. Crocodiles can hold their breath under water for up to 2 hours.

pharaohs ruling over Egypt today, the Nile continues to support life along its banks, providing water and restoring the soil of Egypt's agricultural lands. Every year, snow melts in the mountains of East Africa, sending so much water into the river that the Nile overflows its banks, depositing a black silt, or sediment, that makes excellent **topsoil**.

## The Astounding Amazon

North Americans talk about "the mighty Mississippi," but mighty doesn't even begin to describe the Amazon River, which carries the volume of water of 10 Mississippi Rivers. Combined with its 1,100 tributaries, the Amazon carries the greatest volume of water of any river in the world.

The river starts as a glacial stream high in the Andes and flows more than 4,000 miles (6,436 km) across the South American continent. In places, the river can be as wide as 1 to 6 miles (1.6 to 10 km) during the dry season and 30 miles (48 km) or more across during the wet season. The force of the current, from sheer water volume alone—and the fact that salt water is heavier than freshwater—causes the river water to continue flowing about 125 miles out to sea before fully mixing with the Atlantic Ocean's salt water.

## The Yangtze Is Number Three

The **Yangtze River** in southern China flows for 3,925 miles (6,300 km). It is the longest river in China and the third longest in the world. It originates in the glaciers of Tibet, plunges through limestone gorges, and finally flows into the East China Sea in Shanghai. Every year the Yangtze floods and deposits massive amounts of silt that create fertile plains for farming, especially rice farming. China accounts for 35 percent of the world's rice production, which is a good thing since rice is the staple food for more than a third of the world's population. For thousands of years, the Yangtze has provided transportation and water for manufacturing, irrigation, and household uses, and today a large percentage of China's population lives in the eastern portion of the basin. Uncontrolled flooding, pollution, and destruction of wetlands are all threats facing the river and the people who live along its basin.

## The Mighty Mississippi River

The mighty Mississippi is the centerpiece of the second largest watershed in the world (the Amazon basin is the largest). The Mississippi River begins as a tiny brook, but 2,350 miles

### Wonderful Waterfalls

Waterfalls form when a river flows over layers of hard rock with softer rock underneath. Over hundreds of years, the water erodes the softer rock faster than the hard rock, forming a vertical cliff with a plunge pool at the bottom.

One of the natural wonders of the world, the **Victoria Falls,** also know as Mosi-o-Tunya (the Smoke that Thunders) is located in southern Africa on the Zambezi River between the countries of Zambia and Zimbabwe. The falls are the largest, though not the highest, in the world with a width of 5,604 feet (1,708 m)—that's wider than a mile! It is, alas, a mere 354 feet (108 m) in height.

The honor of being the highest waterfall goes to **Angel Falls** in Venezuela, with a height of 3,212 feet (979 m). The waterfall drops over the edge of the Auyantepui Mountain, and while it doesn't have the official title as one of the "natural wonders" of the world, it is a UNESCO (United Nations Educational, Scientific, and Cultural Organization) World Heritage site—which definitely puts it into the "must visit" category. The height of this waterfall is so great that most of the falling water evaporates into mist or is carried away by winds before it hits the ground.

(3,782 km) later it empties into the Gulf of Mexico, having drained the water from more than 1.2 million square miles (3.1 million km²), including tributary rivers from thirty-three states and two Canadian provinces. One of those tributaries is the Missouri River, which at 2,540 miles (4,087.7 km) in length is actually longer than the Mississippi.

Glaciers formed the Mississippi River basin. The glaciers moved and melted millions of years ago, creating vast **floodplains** in the river valley. These floodplains are still prone to flooding and when that happens, the rising water destroys towns, roads, farms, and anything else that might stand in its way.

## The Holy Ganges

The Ganges River in India is considered a holy river by Hindus. The river begins in the Himalayas and travels through Nepal, India, and Bangladesh on its 1,560-mile (2,510-km) trip to the Indian Ocean. It is the official "national river" of India because of its importance for irrigation, transportation, hydroelectric power, and, especially, its religious significance. Because the Ganges is a special place for those of the Hindu faith, the major religion of India, holy men, widows, and others who have dedicated

themselves to a thoughtful, spiritual life make their homes at the sacred places along the Ganges. They, in turn, attract millions of people who congregate at periodic festivals and fairs.

People who live near the river cremate (burn) the remains of their loved ones on funeral pyres, or flammable objects that are set afloat, burning, on the river. The dying come to the Ganges for a drink from its waters. It is believed that drinking from the Ganges with one's last breath will take the soul to heaven, and that dying by the river can help a person achieve salvation. Some people travel from distant places to immerse the ashes of a loved one in the waters of the Ganges.

But the Ganges is also a river for the living; it is thought that the waters can wash away sin and that a person must dip into the water at least once in a lifetime. With all that dipping, burning, and ash dumping, it is not a surprise that the Ganges River is one of the most polluted and threatened rivers in the world. Inadequate cremation procedures sometimes result in partially burnt corpses of humans and cows, which are sacred animals to Hindus, floating in the river. Less sacred acts also pollute, however. India's

### Flowing Backward

The Tonle Sap River in Cambodia reverses direction every year. Normally, the Tonle Sap flows south, draining into the Mekong River. But when the monsoons (seasonal rains) come, they pour so much water into the Mekong River that it briefly forces the Tonle Sap River to flow backward. The river backs into the Tonle Sap Lake in western Cambodia, which makes the lake grow to more than five times its normal size.

leather industry releases toxic chemicals; millions of gallons of untreated sewage enter the river every day; and dams and irrigation threaten the flow of the river in certain areas. Drinking water from the Ganges has become very risky, although not *too* risky for those drawing their last breath.

### Mother Volga

The Russians call the Volga River "Mother Volga" because of its importance as a source of irrigation, transportation, and

hydroelectric power. At 3,692 miles (2,293 km) in length, the Volga is the longest river in Europe and, impressively, lies entirely within the boundaries of Russia. (There is some debate as to whether Russia should be classified as part of Europe or Asia; see page 68 for more information). More than 40 percent of Russia's people, including half of the country's farmers, live near the Volga and its tributaries.

# AMAZING DAMS

For centuries, humans have built dams on rivers. Dams control water flow to prevent flooding downstream and create reservoirs for water storage.

More recently dams have been built for **hydropower.** The force of the flowing river turns turbines, which generate electricity. The largest hydroelectric dam in the world is the **Three Gorges Dam** on the Yangtze River in China. The Three Gorges Dam is huge: 1½ miles (2.4 km) wide and 610 feet (186 m) tall. The dam creates a reservoir that is hundreds of feet deep and about 400 miles long, big enough to allow freighters to easily navigate the Yangztze. As the world's largest hydroelectric power plant, the dam's turbines can create the equivalent electricity of 18 nuclear power plants. By contrast, the Grand Coulee Dam on the **Columbia River** in Washington State is the largest hydroelectric dam in the United States. It is 5,223 feet (1,592 m) long—less than 1 mile—and 550 feet (168 m) tall.

Hydropower is considered a renewable energy resource, but building dams is not without controversy. For example, creation of the Grand Coulee Dam forced the relocation of more than 3,000 people, including Native Americans whose ancestral lands were partially flooded. The dam also has blocked the migration of salmon and other fish that try to swim upstream to spawn (lay and fertilize eggs). Dams also stop sediment from being carried downstream to create new land.

The Three Gorges Dam brings additional oversize problems. One of the greatest fears is that the weight of the dam may trigger severe earthquakes; the reservoir sits on two major faults.

# FLOODS

Low-lying valleys are great places to live—most of the time—thanks to the lush, fertile soil and the rivers that run through them, providing drinking water, irrigation, and travel. The problem is, river valleys flood. This happens when a river overflows its banks because of a heavy rainfall or rapid melting of snow, or even the collapse of a man-made dam. In addition, humans have covered huge areas of land with concrete, which channels rain into sewers and drains, rather than letting it soak into the ground. This means that water is washed more quickly into rivers.

## Where on Earth Does It Flood?

Your chances of being flooded depend a lot on where you live. Historically, the worst place on earth for flood risk is China. In the last 150 years more than 5 million people have been killed by floods in China. As the polar ice caps melt, higher sea levels and more rain may cause flooding across larger areas and in parts of the world that don't typically flood today.

## Why Are Floods So Dangerous?

You've probably seen images of floods on television. These natural disasters can be very costly, not to mention dangerous. A powerful flood can sweep

everything away, from rocks and trees to cars and houses. Foul-smelling water sweeps into buildings and damages properties. On a bigger scale, everything from roads to crops and electricity lines may be destroyed. Although there's plenty of water around, you wouldn't want to drink it, because it's often contaminated with sewage and could make you very sick. Finding food and clean water after a flood can be a real problem—assuming you can get somewhere safe and dry. Even when floodwater drains away, it can be months or even years before an area recovers.

# LOVELY LAKES

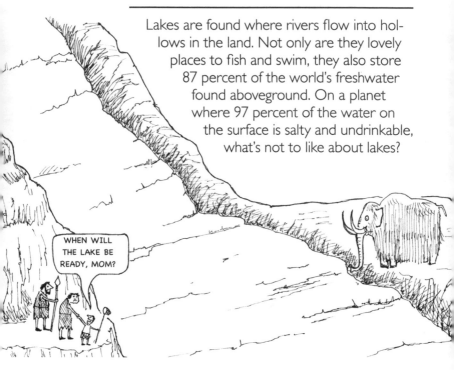

Lakes are found where rivers flow into hollows in the land. Not only are they lovely places to fish and swim, they also store 87 percent of the world's freshwater found aboveground. On a planet where 97 percent of the water on the surface is salty and undrinkable, what's not to like about lakes?

WHEN WILL THE LAKE BE READY, MOM?

## How Lakes Are Formed

Several processes are responsible for creating holes in the ground in which water can collect. Some form in craters made by volcanic explosions (such as **Crater Lake** in Oregon State) or by meteorites striking the earth (such as **Clearwater Lakes** in Canada), but most lakes are formed by the action of glaciers moving on the land.

**Glaciation.** Glaciers are huge blocks of ice and snow that have built up over time. They creep very slowly down steep hills and mountains. As the glacier moves, inch by inch, it scrapes across the earth's surface like an earth-moving machine, digging out boulders and carving into the **bedrock,** or solid rock, that lies beneath the soil.

Around 18,000 years ago, the earth was much colder than it is today, and glaciers covered most of the land. They were continuously growing and moving, gouging holes in loose soil or soft bedrock, depositing material across stream beds, and burying chunks of ice. Later, as the earth grew warmer and the Ice Age ended, the big rivers of ice that had dominated the land began to melt. Over time, the glaciers' meltwaters filled the basins they had carved out, creating lakes.

Glaciers created the world's largest freshwater lake system, North America's **Great Lakes.** The largest of these lakes is **Lake Superior,** on the border between the United States and Canada. It covers 31,700 square miles (82,100 km$^2$)—which is about the same size as the state of Maine. Minnesota, in the northern United States, is known as the "land of 10,000 lakes," but it actually has 12,034 glacial lakes. The Finger Lakes of New York State are also glacial lakes.

**Tectonic Activity.** This describes movements in the plates that make up the earth's crust (see page 13). Tectonic activity can cause the crust of the earth to break into pieces and move apart, forming large holes in the ground called **rift valleys.** When these holes fill with freshwater they form lakes. **Lake Baikal** in Siberia, Russia, was formed in this way 20 to 25 million years ago, making it the **oldest lake** in the world. It is also the world's **deepest lake** at 5,370 feet (1,637 m) deep and contains the largest volume of freshwater on Earth, holding enough water to fill all five of North America's Great Lakes.

Lake Tanganyika in Africa is another rift valley lake and can claim the title of longest freshwater lake in the world.

**Man-Made Lakes.** People have built many artificial lakes, or reservoirs. **Lake Volta,** in Ghana, has the largest surface area of any man-made lake. It is roughly the same size as the island of Corsica in France.

### The Great Lakes of North America

Located on the border between Canada and the United States, the Great Lakes system includes five freshwater lakes: Lake Superior, Lake Michigan, Lake Huron, Lake Erie, and Lake Ontario. Their shores are home to more than 33 million people. Together, the Great Lakes hold more than 21 percent of the world's freshwater. In fact, if you were to pour out the water held in these lakes across the 48 states of mainland America, you'd create a gigantic swimming pool more than 8 feet (2.5 m) deep.

# WHAT MAKES A LAKE A SEA?

Some lakes are even saltier than the ocean. These saltwater lakes form in the same way as freshwater lakes but are missing one key thing—there is no way for water to flow out.

## Bleach-Filled Lakes

One of the strangest lakes in the world can be found in Antarctica. **Lake Untersee** is Antarctica's largest freshwater lake, but its water isn't the kind anyone would want to drink. Thanks to some unusual chemical processes, the water is more like the bleach used to whiten laundry and kill germs in a bathroom than like the water coming out of your faucet. The freezing water of Lake Untersee is permanently covered with ice and is brimming with a gas called methane.

Scientists have recently made an important discovery in Lake Untersee. Although it appeared that nothing could live in the bleachlike waters, they have found a group of tiny, tiny organisms living there. Organisms that live in conditions too extreme for most forms of life are known as **extremophiles.** They thrive in conditions too difficult for most other creatures. If species can exist in Lake Untersee's environment, could there be life on Mars or on the moons of Jupiter and Saturn, which contain similar combinations of ice and methane?

This means that the only way that water can escape is by evaporating into the atmosphere as water vapor. When the water evaporates, it leaves salts and other minerals behind. As time goes on, the amount of salt in these lakes builds up.

Saltwater lakes can be surrounded by land, so why are some of them known as seas? Back in the days of ancient Rome, people decided that all large bodies of salt water should be called seas. So the world's largest saltwater *lake* is called the **Caspian Sea,** even though it is completely surrounded by land. Russia, Iran, Azerbaijan, Turkmenistan, and Kazakhstan all share its shores.

Some lakes are really salty. The saltiest lake in the world is the **Dead Sea** in Israel. It's so salty that almost nothing can live in the Dead Sea's water, which is where the name comes from. However, an astonishing effect of all that extra salt is that you can float effortlessly in its waters!

# ECOLOGICAL COMMUNITIES

# BIO-MAZING

When geographers study life on planet Earth, they divide the world into **biomes.** A biome describes a region with a specific type of climate and the plants and animals that thrive there. Obviously the climate, and especially the amount of rain that falls on an area, has a big influence on which plants will survive in a particular biome. And which plants grow in an area affects which plant-eating animals (**herbivores**) will thrive. In turn, this influences which **carnivorous** (meat-eating) predators will thrive.

There are five major types of biomes in the world: aquatic, desert, forest, grassland, and tundra. You can further divide these biomes into subcategories. Among aquatic (water) biomes, for example, there is a big difference between marine (ocean) biomes and freshwater biomes. Since life began in the ocean with one-celled organisms, let's start there.

## Aquatic Biomes

The **marine biome** is the biggest biome in the world. We are talking about the ocean here, and it covers about 70 percent of the surface of the earth. No one knows how many different plants and animals live in the ocean, but all are dependent on tiny plants like algae and plankton to take in huge amounts of carbon dioxide, release oxygen through photosynthesis, and provide nutrients to other creatures. Fish, mollusks, crustaceans, whales, and more live in the salty water of the oceans (see pages 53 to 56).

The place where freshwater and salt water meet is called an **estuary,** a type of aquatic biome. Estuaries typically are full of plants and animals. Many cities have been built on estuaries (New York City, for example), and in many cases pollution and overfishing have decimated the wildlife that once

## World's Biggest Flower

The world's largest flower blooms in the rain forests of Indonesia. The gigantic titan arum grows up to 10 feet (3 m) high and 5 feet (1.5 m) across. But this isn't a flower to buy for your mother—the blossom supposedly smells like rotting meat and dead bodies. Yuck!

thrived there. **Freshwater biomes** include lakes, ponds, rivers, and streams. Again, algae and larger plants provide oxygen through photosynthesis and food for animals in this biome.

**Wetlands** are an important type of freshwater biome. This is a place where groundwater or rain doesn't drain, and the land stays wet all the time—or for a large portion of the year. Wetlands such as swamps, marshes, and bogs support many plants and animals, help clean the water, control floods, and provide food for humans. The **Pantanal** in South America is the largest wetland of any kind. It is a tropical wetland and is 80 percent underwater during the rainy season. It lies mostly within Brazil but extends into portions of Bolivia and Paraguay, sprawling over an area estimated to be between 54,000 and 75,000 square miles (140,000 to 195,000 km$^2$). That makes it about 10 times larger than the **Everglades,** the largest wetland in the United States. The Pantanal is home to thousands of species of fish, birds, amphibians, reptiles, and mammals, including a healthy population of jaguars, giant anteaters, toucans, tapirs, and capybaras. The Everglades is famous for its bird population, its alligators, and the endangered Florida panther.

## Tundra Biomes

The tundra is a dry, cold, and treeless area. There are two types of tundra, alpine and arctic. Alpine tundras exist above the tree line at the very tops of high mountains. Many peaks in the Alps have alpine tundra, which is where this biome got its name. A handful of peaks in the Appalachians and many mountaintops in the Rocky Mountains have zones of alpine tundra.

The arctic tundra is a flat, treeless swampy plain that extends around the Arctic Ocean in the far north, including northern Europe (Lapland and Scandinavia), Asia (Siberia), and North America (Alaska and Canada), as well as most of Greenland.

Underneath the top layer of arctic tundra soil is a layer of permanently frozen subsoil called **permafrost.** Tree and plant roots cannot penetrate this frozen layer of ground. Above the permafrost is a thin layer of topsoil that thaws in summer, creating many pools, lakes, and marshes that make luxury accommodations for mosquitoes, midges, blackflies, and other biting, stinging insects. The abundant bugs attract more than 100 species of migrant birds, which come for the bug feast each summer. Other animals that live in this biome include polar bears, brown bears, wolves, wolverines, caribou, arctic hare, mink, weasels, and lemmings. Low-growing plants and lichen cover the many rocks on the tundra's terrain. Not many humans live on the tundra.

## Dry, Dry Desert Biomes

When you mention the word desert, do you think of a scorching hot, sandy place filled with camels and palm trees? Hot, sandy deserts make up only about a quarter of the deserts on planet Earth. The rest are cold deserts. A desert is an area of land that receives less than 10 inches (25 cm) of rain or snow during the year or loses more moisture by evaporation or **transpiration** (the moisture given off by plants) than it receives from the sky. Low moisture in the air allows more sunlight to reach the ground, raising daytime temperatures. Large differences in night and day temperatures are a distinguishing feature of a desert. Despite what deserts have in common, the landscape can be pretty different in each one.

**Antarctica.** The world's largest, coldest, and driest desert is the continent of Antarctica. Antarctica receives less than 2 inches (5 cm) of precipitation annually—but all that snow just *never* melts. Over the centuries, the snow has accumulated, and 98 percent of the rocky, barren land of Antartica is covered by a permanent ice sheet. Penguins are the only animals that actually live *on* Antarctica.

WELL, THIS CERTAINLY ISN'T THE TYPE OF DESERT WE'RE USED TO, IS IT, GEORGE?

But the ocean surrounding Antarctica bursts with life, and that's where the penguins feed.

**Sahara Desert.** If you want to find a classic-looking desert, the central part of the Sahara is where you want to go. It has sand dunes 400 feet (122 m) or more in height. The second largest desert in the world, the **Sahara Desert** is the largest *hot* desert. It pretty much covers the northern end of Africa from the Atlantic Ocean in the west to the Red Sea in the east, a distance of some 3,000 miles (4,828 km). In the north, it starts at the Mediterranean Sea and extends 1,200 miles (1,931 km) south, almost into central Africa. It is part of the landscape of the countries of Morocco, Western Sahara, Algeria, Tunisia, Libya, Egypt, Mauritania, Mali, Niger, Chad, and Sudan.

There's no place on earth as consistently hot as the Sahara, which has an average annual temperature of 86°F (30°C). During the hottest months, temperatures can exceed 122°F (50°C). The highest temperature ever recorded in this desert was in Aziziyah, Libya—136°F (58°C).

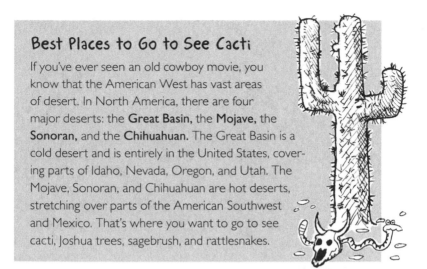

## Best Places to Go to See Cacti

If you've ever seen an old cowboy movie, you know that the American West has vast areas of desert. In North America, there are four major deserts: the **Great Basin,** the **Mojave,** the **Sonoran,** and the **Chihuahuan.** The Great Basin is a cold desert and is entirely in the United States, covering parts of Idaho, Nevada, Oregon, and Utah. The Mojave, Sonoran, and Chihuahuan are hot deserts, stretching over parts of the American Southwest and Mexico. That's where you want to go to see cacti, Joshua trees, sagebrush, and rattlesnakes.

You'd think the Sahara would be a lifeless place, but plenty of long-rooted grasses, cacti, shrubs, and palm trees do survive in parts of the desert. Desert dwellers include camels, of course, as well as antelopes, gazelles, lizards, snakes, and numerous kinds of insects.

**Atacama Desert.** Talk about dry! In parts of this South American desert, no rain has been recorded in the last 400 years. The desert starts at the border of Chile and Peru and stretches southward for nearly 600 miles (970 km) along the Pacific coast. The coastal areas support more life than the interior regions, where vegetation is scarce. Llamas are the most famous animals from this region; they are members of the camel family.

**Arabian Desert.** Another hot desert, the Arabian desert, covers Saudi Arabia, Jordan, Iraq, Kuwait, Qatar, United Arab Emirates, Oman, and Yemen. Parts of this desert are so empty and devoid of life that the Arabs call it the Rub'al-Khali (the Empty Quarter). But other parts of the desert have enough vegetation to support camels, ibex (wild goats), and other grazing animals, as well as plenty of insects, scorpions, lizards, and snakes.

**Gobi Desert.** This barren region of gravel plains and rocky outcroppings is a high-altitude, cold desert in northern China. A portion of the Gobi has just enough vegetation to support camels, wolves, bears, oxen, wild horses, snow leopards, and gazelles. The Gobi also includes areas with no vegetation whatsoever. Overgrazing, soil erosion from wind, and mining activities have all been identified as environmental problems in the region. This desert is expanding, edging ever closer to the capital city of Beijing with mighty dust storms. Desert biomes account for about one-quarter of China's land.

### Desert Dwellers

Trying to survive in a hot desert is tough. On a sunny day in a desert such as the Sahara, the temperature can climb above 122°F (50°C) and fall to below 32°F (0°C) at night. With extreme temperatures like these, people, plants, and animals need to have special ways to adapt to the environment. Cacti and other plants called **succulents** adapt to desert life by storing moisture. A few cold-blooded animals, including reptiles (such as snakes and lizards) and amphibians (such as frogs and toads), are also well adapted to the hot desert. The most famous desert animal is probably the camel, which can make water from the fat it stores in its hump.

### Grassland Biomes

Grasslands are usually found in the middle of continents. They have hot, dry summers and enough precipitation to grow grass but not enough for most trees. Grasslands are

## World's Oldest Tree

Until recently, it was thought that the oldest tree in the world was a 4,700-year-old bristlecone pine named Methuselah, growing in California. Recently, scientists have found a spruce tree in Sweden that they believe has been growing for nearly 10,000 years!

known throughout the world by different names. In the United States they are called **prairies** and extend from the Midwest to the Rocky Mountains. In South Africa, grasslands are called the **veld.** Hot, tropical grasslands called **savannas** are found in South America and Africa. In Europe and Asia, temperate zone grasslands are called **steppes.** In South America, they are called **pampas.**

Grasslands are usually put to use to grow food crops. In the United States, wheat and corn are grown on the prairies, and cattle graze on much of the land. Before settlers converted the grasslands to farmlands and overhunting occurred, buffalo made their home on the prairies. Grazing animals such as rabbits, mice, antelopes, and horses are typical grassland animals. Because grasslands are such open environments, most grassland animals tend to form herds or make burrows in the ground as protection from predators. Today some of the most common grassland animals in North America include prairie dogs, mule deer, coyotes, and wild turkeys. The lion, giraffe, and zebra make their home on African grasslands.

### Forest Biomes

Forests can be found on every single continent, except for Antarctica. They grow almost everywhere—from the hot and steamy areas near the equator to the frosty lands of North America, Europe, and Asia. Climate determines what sort of forest grows where.

**Temperate Forests.** These forests are found in areas where temperatures are fairly moderate and soils rich. **Deciduous trees** such as oak, ash, and maple mostly make up temperate forests. In autumn, deciduous trees shed their leaves, remaining bare during winter. The leaves on the ground decay, and this enriches the soil. Humans have taken advantage of the forest-enriched soil over the centuries, clearing much of the original temperate forests for cropland. Around 5,000 years ago, most of the United Kingdom was covered by forest, but it was

*(continued on page 134)*

**The Rain Forest.** This scene shows a typical rain forest with four layers. Trees and plants need light and space to grow.

**The Understory Layer.** Very little light reaches this layer. Vines called lianas grow around the trees, small ferns, and shrubs. Many insects, spiders, reptiles, and small mammals also call this layer home.

**The Forest Floor.** A mind-boggling variety of creatures, from spiders to pigs and deer to big cats, live in this damp and dark layer.

**The Emergent Layer.** In this layer the tops of the tallest trees, such as mahogany, tower above the canopy and experience strong winds and sunlight. Many birds and insects live in this layer.

**The Canopy.** This tangled layer of dense branches is rich in life, from flowers and fruits to monkeys and birds. It is so thick that it blocks out virtually all light for the vegetation below.

cleared as humans began to use the land to cultivate crops and keep animals. Very little old-growth forest remains in Europe.

In the United States, the deciduous forest is a home for deer, gray squirrels, wood mice, rabbits, and raccoons, to name a few of the critters who live in the temperate forest.

**Boreal Forests.** These forests are found in the cooler northern areas of North America, Europe, and Asia, where the boreal forest is called a **taiga. Coniferous trees** such as pine and spruce make up boreal forests. These trees produce their seeds in cones. Coniferous trees keep their needlelike leaves all year-round, so they are also known as **evergreens.** Many species grow to record-breaking heights. In California, a coastal redwood named Hyperion stands at a colossal 377 feet (115 m)!

Boreal forests are the source for building lumber and paper. The moose is one of the most famous residents of the boreal forest.

**Tropical Rain Forests.** These forests are found in tropical areas around the equator in Africa, Asia, South America, and Australia. Rain forests are warm all year-round and receive about 70 inches (178 cm) of rain a year. They are home to about half of the planet's plant and animal species. There is so much competition for light and space in the rain forest that plants have adapted to living in different layers (see pages 132 to 133).

The **Amazon basin,** roughly the size of the continental United States, is the world's largest tropical rain forest, at 2.5 million square miles (6.5 million km$^2$). It covers about one-third of South America. About 60 percent of this rain forest is within Brazil, another 13 percent lies within the borders of Peru, and smaller areas are located in Colombia, Venezuela, Ecuador, Bolivia, Guyana, Suriname, and French Guiana.

The Amazon is the wettest of the world's rain forests. Heavy rains drench much of the densely forested lowlands throughout the year, but especially between January and June. The vegetation of the rain forest includes a variety of trees, including tropical hardwoods, palms, tree ferns, and bamboos. The trees grow so closely together that their crowns, the parts of the trees that grow above the ground, form a dense canopy. The canopy may soar up to 130 feet (40 m) and is so impenetrable that sunlight seldom reaches the forest floor.

Rain forests sustain vast numbers of different plant and animal species, but the **biodiversity** of the Amazon basin is the greatest of them all, with more species of plants and animals per square mile than anywhere else on the planet. Some of the animals that live in this tropical rain forest are the anteater, jaguar, lemur, orangutan, marmoset, macaw, parrot, sloth, and toucan. Among the many plant species are bamboos, banana trees, rubber trees, and cassavas.

# DESTRUCTION OF THE FORESTS AND CLIMATE CHANGE

In the last 50 years, more than a fifth of the Amazon rain forest has been destroyed. In fact, rain forests all over the world are being cut down. People cut the trees to sell the wood for building homes or making furniture. They also burn the trees to clear the land to grow crops and graze cattle. This affects the planet in many ways.

**Extinction of Species.** About half of all the species of plants and animals on earth live in rain forests. Cutting down the forest means that these species have nowhere to live, so they die out. Scientists believe that the planet is losing up to 50 species each day, many of them from rain forests. If some

animals and plants disappear, others that depend on them to survive will also die out. Humans use many plant species found in the rain forest to make medicines, and the loss of plant species may mean that the chance to find a cure for some diseases may also be lost.

**Global Warming.** Carbon dioxide is a **greenhouse gas** that builds up in the atmosphere. Cutting down forests speeds up global warming because the earth's forests absorb billions of tons of carbon dioxide gas each year. This includes 30 percent of the carbon dioxide humans put into the air with cars and electrical plants. As forests are destroyed, fewer trees remain to absorb the carbon dioxide, and the more greenhouse gases there are in the atmosphere, the warmer the planet becomes.

**Desertification.** The trees and plants in forests hold the soil together and prevent it from blowing away or washing away (erosion). Cutting down forests means that more soil is exposed to the wind and rain, which can lead to more areas becoming deserts.

There are ways to conserve the forests and plant new ones. **Conservationists** urge people to treat forests with respect, to try to reduce global warming before it is too late.

# BIOGEOGRAPHY

In the mid-1800s, Alfred Russel Wallace (1823–1913), a British biologist, anthropologist, and explorer-adventurer was studying the plants and animals on the islands of Malaysia in Asia. He was struck by the sudden differences in bird families he found when he sailed only 20 or so miles east of the island of Bali and landed on the island of Lombok. On Bali he saw birds that were clearly related to the birds that lived on the larger islands of Java and Sumatra and mainland Malaysia. On the island of Lombok, the birds were clearly related to the birds that lived on the islands of Papua, New Guinea and on Australia. He marked the channel between Bali and Lombok as the divide between two regions of animal habitats. He also suggested that the land on either side of the dividing line might have been joined at some point in history.

His discovery was the start of a field of science known as **biogeography,** which looks at the distribution of plants and animals in terms of both regional differences and historical changes in the environment. That line between the two regions—which is now called the **Wallace Line**—actually marks the edge of the Asian continental shelf, and plate tectonics explains the distribution of the species he studied.

It seems that some of the islands on each of the plates were once connected to each other and to the mainland by land bridges. Animals could freely migrate among them, but no such bridge existed between the two tectonic plates. So on each side of the Wallace Line, different families of birds developed.

Biogeography is a new field of study. There are plenty of discoveries yet to be uncovered about how and when and where different plants and animals came to be.

# The World's Most Dangerous Animals

Any animal can be dangerous when cornered, hurt, or protecting its young, but there are animals that are certainly worth avoiding.

**Rhinoceros.** Rhinos are cranky and easily annoyed. Angry rhinos move surprisingly fast and will trample or gore with their horns anyone who has upset them. Rhinos are responsible for approximately 12 deaths a year in Africa and India, although since they are vegetarians, they don't eat anyone they've run over.

**Hippopotamus.** Even crankier than rhinos, hippopotamuses don't have horns, but they do have tusks and they know how to use them, especially when protecting their young. Hippos kill several hundred people a year, so stay out of their way in Africa, where they live.

**Cape Buffalo.** Also known as the African buffalo, this elegantly horned buffalo lives in Africa and kills more humans each year (about 200) than lions do. Another cranky vegetarian, the cape buffalo regards humans as predators and defends itself and its young accordingly, even if the human is armed only with a camera.

**Elephants.** Watch out for the unpredictable elephant if you happen to find yourself in Africa or India. It kills an estimated 300 to 500 people a year by trampling or goring them with its tusks, often for no obvious reason. Its size—the average elephant weighs more than 6 tons—gives it a huge advantage.

**Nile Crocodile.** Despite the specific name, the Nile crocodile lives in almost every major river and body of water in Africa. It kills hundreds of people each year. The danger zone is on the riverbank or lake shore, where a fisherman might be sliding in his boat or a woman might be washing clothes or collecting water. A crocodile attacks by dragging its prey underwater and drowning him.

**Lion.** Who isn't afraid of lions? They kill about 250 people every year. The king of the jungle lives throughout sub-Saharan Africa (except in forests and deserts). Females do almost all of the hunting, working mainly at night and in teams to stalk and ambush prey. Lions live in groups called prides in grassy plains, savannahs, open woodlands, and scrub country—anywhere where they can hide in the vegetation for a surprise attack. The crocodile is the lion's only predator (besides man).

**Scorpion.** Related to spiders, the scorpion is small but venomous. It looks like a miniature crab but has four pairs of legs, a pair of pincers, and a long, segmented tail with a stinger on the end that curls up over its back. Only one type of scorpion that lives in the United States is deadly, but all scorpion stings hurt. Scorpions cause more than 5,000 deaths every year.

**Snake.** Not all snakes bite, but many do and can cause real harm. Snakes cause more than 100,000 deaths every year. Coral snakes, pit vipers, cottonmouths, and rattlers are North American snakes that should be avoided. King cobras are the largest venomous snakes and can be found mainly in southern Asia, northern Africa, and the Philippines. Other species of cobras live in Australia; Papua, New Guinea; and in most of the Eastern Hemisphere.

**Mosquito.** It is hard to avoid mosquitos because they are found on every continent except Antarctica. In terms of the number of deaths caused, the mosquito is number one on any list of most dangerous animals. Mosquitoes in Africa transmit malaria, which results in about 2 million deaths a year. They also transmit viruses such as dengue, encephalitis, and yellow fever. Mosquito bites in North America are very annoying but are mostly harmless.

# INDEX

# Reader's Digest Books for Young Readers

## Write (Or Is That "Right"?) Every Time

Divided into bite-size chunks that include Goodness Gracious Grammar, Spelling Made Simple, and Punctuation Perfection, this book provides quick-and-easy tips and tricks to overcome every grammar challenge.

LOTTIE STRIDE

978-1-60652-341-4

## i before e (except after c)
## The Young Readers Edition

Full of hundreds of fascinating tidbits, presented in a fun and accessible way, this lighthearted book offers kids many helpful mnemonics that make learning easy and fun.

SUSAN RANDOL

978-1-60652-348-3

## I Wish I Knew That

This fun and engaging book will give young readers a jump start on everything from art, music, literature, and ancient myths to history, geography, science, and math.

STEVE MARTIN

DR. MIKE GOLDSMITH

MARIANNE TAYLOR

978-1-60652-340-7